A Visit
Jimmy Brown

By James Stanhope Brown

A factual story of orphan life in the care of Manchester Education Committee and Manchester Corporation between the years of 1936 - 1950

This book is dedicated to all my friends and

colleagues who shared in the

Styal Cottage Homes Experience...

...and more especially, to my sisters

Sylvia and Vera

Also, To Amanda and Lee

Published by
CHRISTINE POTHECARY
Tel : 01832 - 733111
ISBN : 0-9515652-2-2

Printed & bound by
MFP Design & Print

STYAL VILLAGE

CHESHIRE

Dear Jimmy,

You are being most unfair of the Homes,and you know it. We remember you. We, my brothers and sisters, were also not wanted by our Father. You should be ashamed of yourself. Dr. Barnardo got criticised as well, by people like you. Thank God for these places. Where would you and the rest of us be, - IN THE GUTTER. Please send a donation to ANY CHILDRENS HOMES AND GET ON YOUR KNEES.

The above letter was sent to me on the 10th February 1985, following an article published by the Manchester Evening News,in which I made known my intentions to hold a reunion for Styal Homes former inmates. Yes!, I did criticise the Homes, and Yes!, I did suggest they were comparable to a Prison. I also received hundreds and hundreds of favourable letters in acknowledgement, from this country and many other parts of the world. However, out of all those replies, there was just one, which, apart from its lack of sympathy and understanding, caused me to make a decision there and then, that one day, I would tell the world about what did actually 'go on' behind those big iron gates.

The story, (my own story) you are about to read, - 'A VISITOR FOR JIMMY BROWN, is <u>that</u> story.

James Stanhope-Brown

CHAPTER ONE

It was hard not to think of Styal Homes as a prison. The similarities of weekly routines,the discipline and the fear, were everyday reminders of who you were,what you were, and what,if any,your status in life was. Somehow, you survived the trauma of childhood, accepted your fortune or misfortune and when your time came around, departed into the big wide world outside. Such a day had finally come my way on a warm sunny morning in late September during 1949,a few days after my fifteenth birthday. It was sudden,even if the event was a foregone conclusion,once your time was up,so to speak. With -in the short space of thirty minutes or so,following a call to the Superintendents office,I had collected my belongings (that was a laugh),a one way bus ticket to Manchester city centre,and a brown paper parcel containing the necessities of life,such as a suit and a spare change of clothes.Walking through the gates for the last time, I reflected on what the 'Boss' (Superintendent) had said to me just minutes before. "Well,Brown, its time for you to leave us. Go and collect your savings from Matron and ask her for your bus fare to Piccadilly. The bus leaves the village at eleven thirty so don't be late in getting to the cenotaph. When you arrive in Manchester you will be met by the Childrens' Officer. His name is Mr Crossley. Keep your nose clean and remember, you are an ambassador of the Styal Cottage Homes."

For as long as I could remember,I had wished time after time for the day when I could leave Styal and live in Manchester, with a mother and a father in a proper home, with my sisters.

A part of my wish had come true at least. I was now free, free to please myself, free to say what I want, free to indulge in my imaginary world but more importantly,free to enjoy my new found freedom. Suddenly and unexplicably,I was unsure. My brave new world grew momentarily dim on the horizon and the quickening steps of a few moments previous, slowed to a more hesitant pace. I couldn't explain why my future prospectsseemed more insecure than the home I was leaving behind, it just didn't add up. Trying hard to diminish the negative thoughts which were queing with every passing second, I turned my attention to the landscape, a peaceful setting in which there was no hurry,only a gentle nature attending its everyday routine. Setting the pace for the last half mile of Styal and weighing up the plusses in my favour, I began to feel brighter with every warm ray of sunshine. The gates of the Manchester Open-Air School for Delicate Children were wide open as usual and glancing inside, noted the absence of any children. It was always a mystery to me why, as next door neighbours, nobody ever visited us and why, we never had anything to do with them.But of course there were children inside the grounds, as we Styal children knew only too well. Sometimes on certain days of the week, just when 'our mob' were were marching to school in the village, and just when we were passing their gates, a chorus of voices would taunt us with the words -"Styal 'Omes prisoners never get out to eat, Dry bread and water seven days a week" Sometimes the chorus line differed and then it was; "Styal 'Omes convicts been let out today, they marched them 'ere and marched them there and sent them back, 'ooray".It wasn't funny at the time, I smiled inwardly, as I compared their in uendos with my past circumstances.

One of the pluses, in fact one of the biggest pluses was the suit I was wearing. For the first time in my life I had long trousers. They felt awkward and restrictive but if this was what turned boys into men then it was alright by me. I just wish I could show them off to my pals, in fact to any body.There was little chance of that however, Styal at this time of the day, was,apart from the integrated farm noises, devoid of any turbulence. Today, like every other day,Styal was a still and lifeless hamlet, so hushed and tranquil.Only when a motor vehicle passed along the road, as did happen two or three times a day, was the quietness shattered, and in the wake of the receding noise and smoke the village,like an animal in hibernation,simply adjusted itself and returned to slumber. I had better not miss the bus I thought to myself. I was begining to get excited at the thought of climbing the stairs on the bus and sitting on the front seat. Three or four times in my life on different occasions, I can remember the journey made by bus and each time had been an enlightening experience. My suit and my collar were begining to feel very restrictive in the heat of the morning and I half wished that one of those breezes which frequently blew across the Bollin Valley in Carrs Wood, would now sweep across the landscape. Acknowledging the farm activities in the Park's farm and Bailey's farm, I continued along the narrow footpath to the school gates of the Styal Senior

From here, the bus stop was only a hundred yards or so, and in the certain knowledge that the bus hadn't as yet arrived, I purposely lingered near the entrance just in case somebody be it a teacher or a senior boy or girl, could observe my new image. There was no sign of anybody, only the noise of commotion which indicated the lesson being in full swing and without realising, I began to mime the words of a very familiar tune radiating from the classroom. In my minds eye, I could see Smiggy, the school head teacher, pausing between the columns, his cane in one hand, and a rolled-up music book in the other. Remembering the determined manner he adopted as he bounced his powerful bass singing voice to those out of tune, I recalled the fear of those days in which he himself took the class. Momentarily, that same fear resurfaced as I stifled a growing anger, an anger that threatened to spoil a beautiful day. Turning towards the cenotaph, and with a determination that gave added impetus to my walking pace, I made my mind up to forget the school and especially the awesome memory of Smiggy. "I'm free at last", I told my-self. "Free, from all the fear and domination."

The timing couldn't have been better. The large red bus, a double decker with the number 64 emblazoned above the driver drew to an abrupt stop opposite the cottages on Holt Lane. Crossing over to the cenotaph I watched intensely as the ticket collector stepped down from the vehicle and proceeded to indicate to the driver that it was safe to reverse into Station Road. Altering the destination indicators before completing the operation, the engine noise became silenced by the hushed environment. My heightened senses and a high pitch of excitement became the impetus as I devoured the final savoury details of my departure. There was a warm and shimmering heat arising from the bonnet of the engine; there was also the smell of oil and fuel which seemed to indicate reliability and confidence and then,there was the unmistakeable aroma from the warm rubber of the tyres. "Ten minutes before we set off". The shrill voice behind the announcement not only interrupted my daydreaming but shattered my whole being with disillusionment. The conductress, a person whom I had thought previously to be a man, was a woman in a man's clothes. Never in my whole life had I seen a woman dressed in anything other than a skirt or a dress and what befronted me now was a female wearing trousers. Worse than that, she took out a metal box from her breast pocket, extracted a cigarette and a match, and after lighting-up, blew a puff of smoke from her nostrils. My esteem of the opposite sex diminished rapidly as I tried in vain to ignore what I had just witnessed and instead of the intended scampering up the steps of the bus, I slowed to absorb the mixed emotions. This bus was very different to any other I had ridden on, I thought to myself, and instead of the seating being positioned on either side of a centre isle, there were long benches with one access, a sort of gangway running down one side. Breathing in the smell of leather I spread myself on the front seat and took in the panoramic view before me, a view reminiscent of the tree platform in the Bollin Valley, used as a den by the older children. Releasing the brown paper parcel from my sweaty hands and placing it neatly next to the window,I sat back and decided to think of all the things I was going to do when I had a new home in Manchester. Glancing down at the pavement,I could see the driver and his associate sharing a hot drink from a white enamelled billy-can. They appeared to be deeply engrossed in a conversation and at intervals,the driver would pull out a watch which was attached to his jacket lapel."I wonder if anyone else is on the bus", I thought, "it seems such a waste having a bus of this size for just one or two people." Emptying the remains of the tea over the hedgerow, the conductress replaced the lid on the stained billycan, threw the remains of the cig-arette in the gutter, and after a shared joke with the bus driver, made her way to the platform. The bell which sig-nalled the imminent departure of the bus,seemed very signif-icant at that moment. It was almost like an announcement, declaring my termination of life at Styal on the one hand, whilst proclaiming my inauguration into the city of Manches-ter on the other. A swift glance at the Old Ship Inn,now bathed in morning sunlight,became the finale as the bus drew away from the kerb, and holding on to the upright rail for balance, I turned my head for one last glance at the houses along Hollin Lane. With mixed emotions I focused my gaze on the green painted house of number 36, the one where Mr Smith lived,and silently thanked God that I would never see Smiggy again. Only two further landmarks of familiarity remained before leaving Styal, the Monkey tree,now disappearing in the wake of the bus, and the Peacock shaped hedge of Peacock

Farm now looming on the right hand side of the road. The loud noise made by the conductress as she climbed the stairs was enough to interrupt my nostalgia and with a faint hint of excitement I reached into my pocket for the shilling that Matron had given me. This new experience of actually paying for a service was a strange encounter and in excitement, I offered the coin in return for a ticket from the ticket machine. "Where to?" she said, gazing ahead through the window. Now, it was my turn, my big moment as it were. With a courage and confidence that the situation demanded,I proudly pronounced the destination requirements. "The Piccadilly Bus Station, please". The preliminaries of the morning now behind me so to speak, I leaned back in a more comfortable position from where I could take stock of everything before me

Everything had happened so quickly this morning that I had not had chance to allow my thoughts to progress any further than the perimeters of Moss Nook and now, having reached the landmark in question, assured myself that this, was the turning point of my future life. However, before accepting this transformation I allowed myself to dwell on one particular pleasure and one which had been at the back of my mind since learning of my journey into the city. I could feel a tingle as the vision of riding on a real tram through the streets of Manchester grew nearer to reality. For some years now,ever since my sister had taken me out of the orphanage on a visit to a Manchester suburb,I had had a dream of riding on one of those noisy,beautiful red and cream coloured trams. That experience, "the bestest thing that had ever happened in my life", had been so memorable that for weeks and months following, a ride on a tram had become the apex of my wishing list. After Moss Nook came Gatley, and then in sequence were the landmarks of Benchill, Sharston, Northenden and- ? Continuing my line of thought I tried hard to come up with the next destination on the route of the 64 bus, if only to prove to myself how knowledgeable I had become since maturing into adulthood. The bus continued to lurch along the country lanes and the branches of the overhead trees which became shattered by the high vehicle, threw off tiny splinters of sunlight reminding me of the old black and white picures which flickered in the light of a cinema projector. Inevitably the rocking motion from a journey as yet without in cident, produced a change of mood and my sense of expectancy gave way to a feeling of relaxation. It was obvious that my thoughts sooner or later would return to Styal, and as hard as I tried not to let them interrupt my journey into the future, some of the questions simply refused the elimination process. Perhaps now, was the time to seek out the answers to a whole mountain of questions and uncertainties and maybe like John Bunyan, the load would grow lighter with every dis covery and every resolution. The task was too much. I didnt have any answers. Instead, I closed my eyes and sought unconsciousness as the safe option and hoped that sleep would rescue me from having to face the dilemma of a personal investigation.

I wonder if my sister Vera will know about me being let out of Styal? Maybe she will be waiting for me in Piccadilly,I thought, but then concluded to myself that she couldn't know and because my release had happened so quickly, she wouldn't have had time to leave work at such short notice. Vera, the youngest of my two sisters and the one who always referred to me as "our Jimmy",was,in spite of having shared the same Styal experience, still a relative stranger to me, so to speak. The age old custom of segregation between male and female was a principle which ensured the briefest contact possible between brothers and sisters and when reflecting this issue, it all seemed a waste of opportunity. The last conversation I had had with Vera took place several weeks ago in the Carrs Wood in Wilmslow. On that particular day, a Saturday afternoom, she and my eldest sister Sylvia had taken me out of the Homes for a visit to Wilmslow and during our ramble along the banks of the river Bollin, had begun to reminisce about our early childhood in Manchester. In this brief frivolous interlude, Vera reminded me how I came to have the scar on my forehead, an accident which had got her into terrible trouble with our mother. "You were two years old at the time and there was blood everywhere after you fell out of the pram." Sadly, although I didn't take a lot of notice at that time, she presented me with my first in-sight into my early beginings in Manchester and between her revelations and Sylvia's confirming remarks, I learned of how when we lived in Longsight near to Belle Vue,she(Vera) had gone upstairs and found our Mother lying on the floor of the bedroom in front of the fireplace and not moving. Not being tall enough to open the downstairs front door, Vera banged on the window in panic, trying to attract attention from the neighbours in the street and screaming all the time "mi' Mother's dead." With no rewards from the window knocking, she and Sylvia moved a chair to the front door and climbed successfully to the latch before finally running out into the street in panic. The neighbours quickly responded to the screams of "mi' Mother's dead" from both the girls and in no time at all an ambulance and a police turn-out filled the street with onlookers. Glancing at my sisters as they narrated the unfortunate episode I noticed Vera wiping her eyes with her coat sleeve. "It wasn't funny at the time she said, "I remember us all going in the ambulance to the Crumpsall Hospital and that kind neighbour Mr Taylor sitting us on his knee and offering us a comforting arm whilst we sobbed and yelled aloud." For some reason Sylvia added few comments and seemed to rely on Vera for verification of the story. "The next thing we knew", went on Vera,"we were put in the back of another ambulance along with two large women who both wore white apron uniforms and big white hats covering their heads. We were still yelling when we reached Moss Side, an unfamiliar part of Manchester,and in spite of being told to "shut-up" we kept on shouting:"we want our Mother." The place we went to was called Elmfield. It was like a big house with high walls and high windows and it frightened us more when we were taken in and the doors locked behind us. I remember you Jimmy, being taken away into another room and me and Sylvia screamed all the more. This time it was"I want mi'brother, I want mi'brother." Whether it was because we were screaming too loud or because we had got hysterical I dont know but the next thing that occurred was being pushed over a sink and being told that unless the crying stopped, the bar of carbolic soap in her hand would be pushed into our mouths and "that would shut us up." When me and Sylvia were finally put to bed it was in a room with bars at the windows, and in the claustrophobic darkness of that night, we both sobbed ourselves to sleep over losing our Mother and our baby brother."

Vera, Jimmy, Sylvia.

C H A P T E R   T W O

My sisters never did tell me how we actually made the final journey to Styal but then I had never really been interested in finding out. To me, the Styal Cottage Homes was all I had ever known from childhood and had begun, ...I searched my memory for recollections of my early days in the orphanage but most of it was blank. Babyhood in the Styal Homes seemed to have been a very brief affair and yet, apart from the usual associations with potty's, cots and bottled milk, one connection had remained in my mind as if indented. I can almost smell the gentle fragrance from the tall hedgerows surrounding the playing fields as my mind began to drift back to all those years ago. I was wearing some kind of white uniform which also included a white bonnet for protection from the hot sun. The field was a mass of buttercups and daises which projected a beautiful panorama of colour, and in this hushed sea of tranquility I experienced a glowing feeling of peace and contentment, as yet without equal.Child hood, I concluded, in its oblivion and ignorance, was a safe world where peace and serenity appeared to harmonize with the country garden of Styal. It was this stillness and qietness which, along with the remoteness of the Dean Valley colony, that had inspired me to believe that at the peak of my infancy, time literally did stand still. The calm of my childhood ended at precisely 10.am on a Monday morning sometime around early summer of 1939. I remembered being taken for a walk -a distance of little more than two hundred yards - by a lady who was addressed as Matron, who, with a display of authority, explained about the 'big boy's' home in which

I was now going to take up residence. "Your new Mother is called Miss Chedley and the name of your new house is 'Nut' Cottage" Releasing my hand to knock on the door, the Matron continued with more chatter and finally concluded with a statement that since I was now a big boy and going to live in a big boy's home, I would have to be on my best behaviour for my new mother. The door opened and Matron pulled me in over the step. "Well, Miss Chedley, what do you think of our new boy then? His name is Jimmy Brown and little Jimmy is going to be a good boy for you." Miss Chedley, an elderly looking lady wearing a long blue overall beneath a starched white apron, took me by the hand and sat me down at the kitchen table. "Would you like some cake and milk" she said. I nodded my head in silence. "Don't be shy" said Matron."When your new mother asks you a question, you say; yes Mum." By the time I had munched the currant bun and drunk a mug of milk Miss Chedley and Matron were at the front door exchanging goodbye's or whatever it was. "Don't forget what I said to you" said Matron as she turned for one last look."I shall ask Miss Chedley if you're being a good boy." That over,Miss Chedley took me by the hand and said;"I'm going to show you round your new home whilst the older boys are out." Leading me out of the kitchen and into a much larger room she said; "this is the dining room come playroom and this, -pointing to a raised chair- is where you will be sitting so that I can keep an eye on you." Timid and fretful, my eyes wet from tears of uncertainty,I clung on to Miss Chedleys hand as she led me up the wide wooden staircase. "We have three bedrooms and a bathroom." Pausing at the top of the landing, she turned into a room which appeared to be full of beds. "This is the big boys bedroom, isn't it nice and tidy?" I gazed at the polished linoleum and my stare continued along each leg of the rows of iron bedsteads. Turning in the opposite direction she then nudged me along the corridor to another room which was referred to as No.2 bedroom. Again, the same clinical smell and the same uniformity, the only difference being,the size of the room, with only six or seven beds. "Now we'll show you where your bedroom is." With my hand firmly grasped in hers she entered a room similar in size to the first one and led me to a bed which was situated underneath the window and second from the end wall near the fireplace. Lifting me up and sitting me at the foot of the bed, she explained that out of the ten beds in the room, my bed place was number seven. "I will come and tuck you up in your bed tonight but I want you to watch what the other boys do. Remember, when you go to bed it is to sleep, and when the light goes out there musn't be a sound." The memories of my early days in the 'big boys' home are not as distinct as they once were but on reflection, I can bring back to mind that first introduction and initiation into what was to be my home for the next nine or ten years. At teatime that same evening, Miss Chedley led me into the dining room and sat me on a high chair near to the open fireplace, telling me to "pay attention and listen carefully to the way we do things and you will soon fit into our family." The routine of the home and its occupants was such that it was virtually impossible not to become involved in the daily duties of household domesticity and, as I observed from my first meal time, every boy -from big ones to little ones- seemed to play some part in the clockwork proceedures. The introduction over, the prayers chanted, the meal tables cleared of every last crumb,and and the room converted to its former state, was the finale to what had been a very busy day. "Bedtime for little boys" I had been informed, was 6.pm. "For the older ones, it was 7 pm, and the 'big' boys bedtime was 8.pm." The smell from the warm pyjamas which until a few moments ago had been hanging from the ceiling rack above the stove, contrasted sharply with the cold starched sheet on the bed. Tucking me in and telling me to go to sleep, Miss chedley promised to come and look in on me when the other boys came to bed. "Seeing that this is your first night in your new home, the window blinds can stay open until later." The excitement and anticipation of sleeping in a big boy's bed overruled the sadness which had accompanied me up the stairs and to prove to myself just how grown-up I had become, I tried to touch the frame of the iron bedstead with my toes. Sleep did eventually take over, but not before I had become familiar with the noises from the other children of the house and the constant comings and goings of the swallows, who's nests under the eaves, lay directly above the window. After several weeks of being a new boy of 'N' Home, the settling-in period eased with every intake of routine and it wasn't long before I was playing my small part in the daily and weekly proceedures of homecare.

Towards the end of summer, an excitement of sorts had breath -ed new life among the occupants of the home and a new word was added to my vocabulary; 'holiday'. The annual holiday migration for all the boys and girls from Styal Homes during 1939 was to the Welsh coastal resorts of Colwyn and Abergele and somewhere in a tiny corner of my mind, I can remember a wooden chalet and an open meadow in which a discarded old railway carriage served as a fantasia for all the would-be engine drivers. Halfway through my first ever holiday and two weeks before my 5th birthday, a dark invisible cloud set -tled on the whole camp and the word 'war' was pronounced in every other sentence. Hurriedly and dejectedly, a hasty re-treat was made back to Styal and all thoughts of recreation were quickly replaced by a mood of extreme depression. Sum-mertime, and holidays and picnics in Styal woods were now a thing of the past as the stern and sombre mood of wartime be -gan its infiltration of everything and everybody. Overnight or so it seemed, an army of workmen appeared in the colony and amidst a great deal of excitement on the part of all the children,began digging-up the vegetable plots in order to lay their foundations. A few weeks later, after an input of tons of steel and concrete had been swallowed up by the man-made craters, the landscape became dotted with the new 'dug-outs' or, as Miss Chedley pointed out, "air raid shelters." At sometime during the preparation for war, and a birthday which went unnoticed, I began my first term at Styal Junior School and with it, a routine which was to dominate my world for the next two years. The school, a low red brick building which contained four classrooms, was situated opposite the Styal Homes Church and lay a distance of approximately one hundred yards from my house. Each morning, after the breakfast and jobs rota had been complied with,a bugler boy would sound the 'reveille'on his trumpet and all the girls and boy -s would come out of the houses and make their way to the appropiate parade ground. In the case of the infants and juniors, the playground served as the meeting point and on command from the whistle blown by a grownup,the boys separat -ed from the girls. Harvest festival, I was to conclude a few years later, always coincided with the onset of dark and long evenings, and it was during my first experience of this spectacle when the church seemed to be overflowing with all manner of vegetables, sheaves of corn and masses of flowers, - it happened.The loud whirring noise which drowned out the church organ signalled the commencement of the newly install -ed Styal Homes early warning system. For the next 5 years, the new siren which had been strategically placed on the roo -f of the main office building,would not only inform all the Styal locality of an impending air-raid, but would also add a new dimension in terms of fear, to the children of the col -ony. The parade ground opposite the Superintendant's office normally only used by the older school children, became the focal point of an assembly of all the children of the Styal Homes. Using a megaphone, the 'Boss', (Superintendant) dressed in military style uniform with tin hat and poncho cape and a rifle slung over his shoulder, stepped-up on his dias and addressed the gathering of home-mothers and children. In a sombre mood and spelling out his message loud and clear, -a scene which was to be repeated at frequent intervals during the next few weeks- he went through a whole list of do's and dont's allied to the early warning siren and the follow-on 'all clear' siren.Many of the new rules were an extention to the institutionalism already in place and it was only by mentioning other aspects of war such as how to use gas masks and air-raid shelters that the interest of the children was rekindled. Back at the Home, Miss Chedley and her assistant revealed a further set of rules designed to assist in the efforts of the nation to combat the growing food shortages. "We have all got to make sacrifices" she said, "and from now on,there will be no wasting of food whilst other people less fortunate are starving." The onset of colder weather and pitch black night-times seemed certain to extend what looked like being a long dark winter ahead. The first casualty of the war so to speak was a nine year old girl who lived about fifty yards opposite to me in the house known as 'B' Home. According to rumours at that time, this girl had committed a very bad offence,so bad in fact that all the children of the Homes had been summoned to assemble at the parade ground. On that day, a Saturday prior to the Easter festival, a mass of attentive children and staff faced the windows and doors of the administrative building in anticipation of the Superintendant's arrival. In this hushed setting, the groups of 5 and 6 year olds were told to sit on the ground so that the older children could have a better vantage of the proceeding At the rear of the parade the Styal woods sloped down to the river below and as ever,the surrounding trees were alive to the shrill choruses of the crow population who's constant cawing became a loud echo in the silence of the ensuing drama.

The coldness of the kerb on the back of my legs sent a wave of shivers which resulted in a teeth chattering episode and a strong desire to return to the hot stove in the kitchen of 'N' Home. Dressed in some kind of military uniform,the Boss made his appearance and was closely followed by the Matron who's outstretched hand was firmly attached to the arm of a young girl. Blowing on his silver coloured whistle to ensure maximum attention he began his introduction as to the reason for the present circumstances. "As you all know, there is a war on, and as has been explained to you, there are very strict rules to be followed. This girl -pointing to the small figure held tightly by Matron- has broken one of those rules, and because of the seriousness of the offence, is now going to recieve a punishment." The young girl,now pulling away from her superior in an attempt to escape the wrath, began crying as the Boss continued. "Last night, this girl opened the blinds in her bedroom and because the lights were still on, allowed a beam of light to shine out into the dark sky. It was only by luck that the beam was not spotted by an enemy aircraft otherwise, we may have been bombed. To teach this girl a lesson and to make sure that nobody else makes the same mistake, I have instructed Matron to punish her in full view of everyone." The silence, interrupted only by the noises from the tree inhabitants, had an eerie feel as everyone present witnessed the frightened girl being made to bend over. In the subdued hush, the cane landed across bare buttocks and in consequence, the screams of the recipient increased accordingly until on the sixth and final stroke the Boss intervened with a - "let that be a lesson to everyone." In future years I, like most other Styal residents, would look back at that incident and gauge its impact in terms of fear and the bearing on future behaviour. However, for myself the drama was not yet concluded and another decade was to pass before it was revealed to me that the frightened girl I had witnessed in the 1940 parade ground incident was no other than my older sister Sylvia Brown.

1940, was in some ways the the begining of my life, for in terms of memory everything seemed to progress from a year fraught with excitement, fear, and emotional turmoil. Vivid, to say the least, was my fear of the sirens which not only increased as the weeks went by, but turned night-times into nightmares. Half awake and half asleep, I shivered my way with all the other children into the air raid shelters where the cold darkness and smell of oil lamps infiltrated every intake of breath. Squashed between all the other boys and numb with a mixture of coldness and apprehension, I tried to take an interest in what the older and more knowledgeable boys were telling each other about the type of aircraft that was allied to the engine noise overhead. Being too young to understand the technicalities of military warfare, I chose my own iterpretation of which aircraft were which by the assumption that the noise from the heavy bombers was allied to the deep continuous drone, whilst the lighter and faster air craft identified themselves with a higher pitched tone and a faster engine revolution. "Is everybody accounted for" said the Boss as he forced his large frame through the dug-out doorway. His entrance silhouetted behind the torchlight on the cold concrete walls,brought a warm feeling of strong re-assurance and with the additional regalia of tin helmet and rifle, all doubts and insecurities became dispelled. There was always an upsurge in morale whenever the Boss did his rounds, and if it had not been for his strong sense of duty and encouraging sing-songs during the bombing armadas, life in the air raid shelters would have been very intimidating.

Styal bomb site.

CHAPTER THREE

After what seemed an eternity, my two years of infant and junior education drew to a close and the summer holiday of 1941 gave a beckoning promise of hot sunny days and hours of playing-out on the large recreational field. Gone forever, or so I hoped, were the long days in the classroom and the never ending choruses of; A is for Apple, B is for Bear,C is for...., and so on and so on. Also I hoped, was the end in sight for the endless hours of recitation of the arithmetic tables although intuition implied that this was purely wishful thinking. Thoughts of going to the Senior school after the holidays had now taken root to such an extent that the implications of my promotion brought home to me the meaning of what being a 'big boy' (Miss Chedley's expression)really meant. Bang' My head hit the wall of the corridor as I bent down to avoid a clout aimed by the new assistant housemother and whilst assessing the singing noises and the reasons behind the onslaught, another blow -this time from a shoe- was aimed at my back. "I'll teach you to wet your bed, you just wait, if it happens again Brown, you'll get another hiding. Do you hear?, say something." Sobbing,and determined not to give way to the tears, I replied; "yis M'm." "Are you going to behave yourself? There's no playing out and staying-up for you tonight.You can go to bed early and no supper.Do you hear?" "Yis M'm," I repeated quickly to avoid any further punishment. Going to bed early, the same time as the very young ones, whilst losing out on an hour's playing-out time, was a far worse punishment than being thrashed with the shoe or whatever else she used. My pride dented, and thoughts of my pals playing out without me and then having a slice of bread and dripping for supper became unbearable as I stared at the bare walls from my bed. How I hated Miss Chedley for going on holiday and leaving Miss Albert in charge. It wasnt my fault I wet the bed. Miss Chedley, who regularly woke me every night for the toilet, had once said to me that one day soon I would grow out of the habit and she wouldn't have to spank me any more. Fortunately,although I hadn't appreciated until now, Miss Chedley's spanking with the warmed-up black galosher, normally hung on a nail by the side of the stove, had become such a commomplace routine that I accepted it all without fuss, and like the telling-off, absorbed each punish -ment and hardened myself for the next one. "Tonight, I'm going to say a very special prayer to Jesus." My thoughts became more active and louder as I thought about my new plan of action. "I'll wait until Miss Albert has been in all the bedrooms and woken the children for the toilet and then,when she has completed the rounds,I'll climb out of bed and kneel down and ask Jesus to forgive me for being naughty,and in re turn I will stop wetting the bed." In the excitement of having found the obvious solution to my problem, the night,with its routine of toilet training,passed in the usual state of stupor and my resolution like myself, became chrysalised, neither awake nor asleep. The early morning sunshine which poured into the bedroom from behind the drawn blinds should have heralded the begining of another exciting day of adventure and high expectations. Suddenly, with the realization that I had failed yet again to wake-up with dry sheets, my sunny optimism from a few moments ago disappeared under a large black cloud and my immediate future became too awful to contemplate. My anxiousness at the prospect of being discovered by Miss Albert caused me to tremble, and in a cold state of fear, my teeth began to chatter uncontrollably.When the moment did arrive and the bedclothes were ripped off, I found it impossible to contain myself any longer and replied with an outburst of loud sobs. Perhaps it was this display of early morning emotion in front of a bedroom audience that silenced Miss Albert or,maybe my outburst had knocked her,at least for the moment, off balance.Whatever the reason, I con -sidered my escape to be a miracle. "Don't think you've got away with it Brown, I want you in my corridor this afternoon before teatime." The hairbrush in the housemother's hand came perilously close to reigning down a string of blows and but for my escape under the beds,would have connected on my head and shoulders. In a state of dejection the rest of the day weighed heavy under the knowledge that I was living on borrowed time and my nervousness increased with every minute that ticked its way towards the teatime rendezvous. Never, had an air-raid warning siren sounded so musical,and instead of the usual fear and trembling as I rushed with all the oth -er children to assemble for the dug-outs, I breathed a sigh of relief in the knowledge that the air-raid would eliminate the impending punishment. I couldn't dare whisper what was going through my mind but secretly, as I sat in the crowded shelter clutching my gas mask, I was glad that the German bombers had chosen the late afternoon instead of the night-time. Little did any of us in the shelters realize that to-day's air raid would forever be regarded as Styal's most significant day of the 2nd world war. Perhaps the loud bang -more of a loud thud, I thought- which accompanied the bomb-ing, should have indicated the severity of the raid on Ring-way aerodrome but being naive of everything that occurred outside the gates, one could only wait until rumours reached the Homes in the weeks to follow.Much to the surprise of all the children,the next day brought with it,a command from the Boss for a special parade, which was to include the staff of the entire Homes.

I can still see him now. The rocking and swaying motion from the seemingly endless bus journey ensured my anchorage to my roots as my thoughts returned to the 'line-up'at the colony. "Attention,Attention." With an amused recollection of that day, I recalled his military manner as he stepped on to his dais to address the under-age army under his command."As you all know, the air raid which gave us grave concern yesterday was an attempt by the German Airforce to bomb our aircraft industry whilst disrupting operations at Ringway Aerodrome. Fortunately, on this occasion,the Germans were unsuccessful, but the bombs which failed to hit their target landed not far from here and caused considerable damage and some loss of life. I have to remind you all that there is a war on and every instruction concerning air raid drill must be implemen-ted in full." Leaving Matron to carry out the remainder of the proceedings the Boss, still attired in his poncho cape and carrying his rifle and tin helmet, retired to his office looking weary from his responsibilities. According to the 'true' story being passed from one boy to the next, and seemingly told to eager audiences throughout the colony,a german bomb, the one which had been heard exploding during yesterday's air raid,had fallen just outside the Homes perimeter,at the bottom of Twinney's Brow, and the crater it had made was so huge that a lake had formed at the point where the Bollin joined the river Dean. So vivid was the tale of the bomb crater and the consequential flooding of the Carrs Woods that sleep that night became a nightmare with floods, shipwrecks, and drownings becoming intertwined with the day to day discipline of Styal Homes. Another day, another routine and another good hiding. Today,there was no escape from the hairbrush in the hands of Miss Albert. Scarcely had the sheets been ripped off when a barrage of blows landed across my back, buttocks and legs, causing me to tremble not only from the fear of physical punishment but also the indig -nation at being singled out in front of my room-mates. How I wish Miss Chedley would hurry back from her leave.

On reflection, I don't remember much about my seventh birthday. Maybe because of the war and the rationing and other re strictions, birthdays weren't allowed. My time had come,so to speak, and with it all the new responsibilities connected with the crucial second stage of one's life. "New learning is a major part of the Senior School education, and the discipline is of more importance," - so said the Boss in one of his pre school commentaries. My first weeks at the Senior School in Styal were full of learnng and excitement and generally growing up, making new pals,and tasting the limited freedom outside the colony. I had never worn boots until now but included in the winter clothing issue was a pair of big black boots complete with iron studs and horseshoe heels. It had been my wish for longer than I could remember,to wear a pair of boots for the sole purpose of making sparks by skimming the road surface, just as the older boys did. Perhaps my enthusiasm for school was due to the new routines,the new teachers,and probably, the new curriculum; everything about it seemed to be so inspiring especially the geography and history lessons. The war was never far away and the autumn of 1941 seemed to be a never ending succession of air raid drills, so much so,that schooling on some days was cancelled due to the long nights in the shelters. By the onset of win -ter I had become integrated into the Junior system of the school which, if anything,appeared to be no different than its senior counterpart. The daily school routine began with the revellie at 8-30am, played by a member of the Styal Band and with military precision every senior schoolboy or girl would make a hurried dash to the parade ground where eventually they would line up in columns for an inspection before the march to Styal. On command from the Boss, Mr Dirkoff the bandmaster would mount his bicycle and give his instructions to the crocodile formations. Over the approaching years I would become so familiar with the school march that I, like every other member of the group,would get to know every inch of the pavement, even in a blindfold. The first landmark out side the gates was the little orchard which, apart from the glut of small apple trees,contained a gooseberry harvest that produced the best tasting gosseberries in Styal. Next, came the entrance gates of the Open Air School adjoining the Styal Homes Farm known locally as Park's Farm. Across the main road and up the cobbled pathway was another farm associated with the orphanage called Bailey's Farm, an establishment known more for its juicy apples than its milk and eggs. From this junction the road to the school was a continuous footpath, straight in line and flanked on either side of the road by prickly hawthorne hedges. Just prior to the school gates and almost hidden by the overhanging trees lay a dirt path which led to another of the village farms who's title hung from one of the overhanging branches and displayed the name;'Hope's Farm'. Once inside the school gates the boys made a bee-line for the playground to the right of the building, whilst the girls likewise, turned in the opposite direction to enjoy a brief play session before the whistle blew time-up.

"There was a time," said Miss Chedley, whilst relating the traditions of Styal Homes and of how severe the discipline used to be before the arrival of Mr Dirkoff,- "when children under the jurisdiction of Mr Cochran, the bandmaster,used to march to school in a proper formation, and not the slovenly way that Mr Dirkoff allowed. Mr Cochran was a proper soldier who commanded respect , and woe betide anyone who disobeyed" Thank goodness Mr Cochran had left the Homes as I was arriving,I thought to myself. His departure from the village had been the talking point amongst the older children for what seemed an eternity,but that was probably due to his overwhel-ming reputation and his long associations with the village and orphanage. Some of the senior boys and girls still test-ified to their claim of having been caned severely on the backs of their legs by Mr Cochran for marching out of step to and from school. Walking up and down Styal Road four times a day during school days gave one plenty of thinking hours,and thoughts of Mr Cochran came and went like almost any other topic. In the main, most thoughts were allied to the war,and especially on the days when the siren sounded and the crocodile formation had to take cover or run to the nearest shelter. One thing I had noticed since starting the senior school, was the increasing number of barrage balloons dotted about the skyline,mainly over distant Ringway. Initia-lly,I assumed them to be hazards which, on command,would be propelled upwards to form a barrier against incoming enemy aircraft. To this day,I am still unsure of my assumption but one thing I am certain about is their use as a parachuting platform. The first time I spied the tiny figures falling to earth from the sky was both a surprise and revelation,and it was only when the parachutes opened that I realized the true implication of being at war. During the months that followed whilst walking to school, I would often search the skies in the direction of Ringway and sometimes my efforts would be rewarded with the appearance of a parachutist. Unfortunately my excitement was short lived and within that year, the par-achutists along with the barrage balloons,had disappeared from the Styal landscape. During the ensuing years at Styal it would be made known to me by Mr Lyle,that the reason the parachutists left the local area in preference for a place called Tatton Park,was because of the many injuries sustained on the hard tarmac of Ringway Aerodrome.

After a few months of senior school and fast approaching my 7½ birthday I had decided that in infinite wisdom, Saturday was by far the best day of the week. This was the day when, after breakfast and having completed the work rota, the mantle of claustrophobia dispersed. This was the day when the weekly traumas disappeared, at least for the time being, and were replaced by an overwhelming feeling of freedom and exhilaration. Once outside the confines of the Home,the day's prospects conjured up a mythical magical wonderland, ranging from the exploration of the surrounding woodland,the crossing of the river Bollin,the search for wild animal life and, a host of great adventures waiting to unfold. Unknown to me, this particular Saturday had already passed the planning stage and my destiny now lay in the hands of a group of older boys belonging to Nut Cottage. Begging to go along with them and promising 'not to tell',the small group converged on the playing fields where eventually a football game of sorts began between 'them' and 'us', them, being some lads from another home. Looking back down the years and reliving that first adventure, brought a smile to my face. It would seem that because of the war, the curfew which prevented children from venturing outside the gates was still in force. However, the quest for adventure and the determination on the part of the older boys to explore the Bollin for pieces of shrapnel, had resulted in a plan of action which "could not fail". Listening to the scraps of conversation, I became convinced by the simplicity of it all. What could be more innocent? Within a very short period from kick-off, the ball fell onto the main road 'by accident', and because it landed on the apex of the steep hill, continued to descend at a quickening pace down Twinney's Brow and in the direction of Wilmslow. Inevitably,a mad scramble to retrieve the ball got under way and climbing through the hedgerows,the well informed gang set off to rendezvous at the spot where the ball was destined to stop; the bomb crater near to the National Trust wood gates into Styal Woods. My dreams of a flooded Bollin valley a few weeks weeks ago,was now a disappointing myth. There were no signs of the Bollin or the Dean having been in flood but true to local rumour,the huge bomb crater now brimming with water was a compensation which brought back vivid memories of the consequencies of the air raid. In no time at all a barrage of pebbles and grass sods were thrown into the pit with the accompanying guesses as to how deep the water was. It soon became obvious from the excited shouts from my pals that in order to prove a point,a measuring device of sorts was required. The old gnarled and knotted stumps dotted on the hillside were the most likely choice but they were too heavy and too short and in any case, would have taken-up too much valuable time. One of the bigger lads' pointed to the woods inside the National Trust and commanded everyone to help carry the long tree branch over the stile. With everything going to plan and my thoughts engrossed in what the long branch would yield beneath the murky waters,I failed to make a quick response to the whistle which was sounding some where close by. "Police!, Scram!." By the time I realized what the fuss was about,most of the boys had fled in panic either into the woods or in the direction of Pownall Park and the Carrs. Deciding on a different route of escape,I ran towards Styal Road with the intention of hiding along the river bank under the bridge but in the confusion I bumped in to a man walking his dog. Marching back to the Homes up the steep hill gave me time to reflect on the manner in which a total stranger had apprehended me and then handed me over to the policeman. "It wasn't fair. It was none of his business." What was going to happen to the five of us who had been rounded up was of more consequence and I became very frightened at the prospect of a punishment. My stomach churned with the cold fear as we marched through the gates and told to stand to attention outside the Boss's house. It was mid-day now, and I could smell the food from the nearby homes and visualized the concern on the homemother's face at the empty seats at the dinner table. Aware that I was hungry and fatigued, I prayed inwardly that Boss Huggins would deal with us later, a prayer which was almost immediately answered as the Boss broke off his conversation with P.C. Waite and ordered us to report to his office at 2.0.o'clock sharp. The danger over, at least for the moment,brought a huge sigh of relief as the tense limbs became relaxed, and in the mad scramble to salvage whatever was left on the dinner table,the noon appointment became temporarily forgotten.

CHAPTER FOUR

If Saturdays were adjudged to be the nearest thing to complete and utter freedom, then Sundays must have counted as the most confining and sombre day of the week. According to the Homes vicar,Sundays were for rejoicing and giving thanks and celebrating the day of rest which had been granted to us However,during my younger days in Styal,Sundays heralded the start of another six days of restrictions and fears and, another six days of despair and hopelessness. Breakfast over, prayers chanted and jobs of work completed,the day's routine began with a change of clothes where Sunday suits replaced the everyday school attire. After a final inspection by the home-mother for cleanliness and tidiness,the crocodile formation in answer to the tolling from the church bell,would join up with all the other Home groups en-route for the subdued walk to the Church. No talking,was the order of the day as the morning assembly filed through the gates,and woe betide any child who showed any form of behaviour other than Sunday observance. After what seemed like an eternity and with a great inward sigh of relief,the hour long service was brought to its conclusion. If there was any respite in the Sunday routine it occurred immediately after the heavy wood doors had swung open to allow the well ordered exit of the hundreds of children and their superiors. Stage two of the day's routine was probably the highlight of the day, especially for those younger ones like me who had felt the heavy suffocation during the service. Another crocodile formation but this time with a mood and pace which adjusted to a landscape already tranquilized by the Sunday observance.This was the moment when every housemother and her respective brood made their way to the front gates of the colony to prepare for a walk around the outskirts of Styal village, a scene enacted week in and week out and probably,since time began at the orphanage. The Sunday walks alternated according to the whim of the Home-mother and the weather. Sometimes there was just a stroll around the village of Styal but on most occasions the destination lay in the direction of either the Carrs Wood leading to Wilmslow Parish Church or, the Carrs Wood higher level walk to Lindow Common. One other walk, and perhaps the most popular,was the longer route through Styal Woods,a journey which skirted the river Bollin and Greg's Mill and culminated on Altrincham Road at Styal village. In keeping with Miss Chedley's interpretation of the Sabbath, lunch was observed in very subdued tones with no-one daring to break the silence other than to chant a Godly verse for the food on the table. In the stifling atmosphere of the so-called 'quiet period',having completed the work rota and imbibed in a game of snakes and ladders,it was time for Sunday School at the Church,an event requiring yet another orderly procession. If Sundays did hold any compensation it was in the evening teatime meal. As opposed to the weekday meals, when every serving was a "good for you" menu and the diet had to be eaten,like it or not, the Sabbath teatime appeared to cater for the popular likes of every individual child. Sometimes,on the odd occasion and if Miss Chedley thought we had earned it with good behaviour,a second helping of bread and dripping or bread and jam or even an extra helping of custard was the reward. Fortunately,for myself and the other younger children who were in the early bedtime cateogory,the day was almost ended,whereas for the older inmates of the house,another church service had yet to be endured.

By the time I had reached my eighth birthday I began to realize that Styal Homes was not a home in the normal sense of the word. My intuition had also told me that our exist-ence in the colony was very different to the people living on the other side of those big gates, and as the comparisons of 'them' -on the outside- and 'us'-on the inside- grew more stronger,so too did my evolving sense of inferiority. It was probably at this stage of my life that I developed the habit of making wishes,either under my breath or out loud,and as my technique improved with the years so too did the observ-ations from Miss Chedley who, in her less austere moments, would address me as 'Jimmy Wish Wish'. A half smile crept over my face as I looked back at my time in Nut Cottage and recalled the times when Miss Chedley would tut-tut at my hab -it and imply that I was wishing my life away. In her unguar -ded moments there was a faint hint of motherly instincts which seemed to suggest that she had a soft spot for me. How -ever, I was in trouble more times than I was out of it and what with the other twenty seven boys of the family,the har-sher side of her nature was always more predominant. In my opinion,'Jimmy Wish Wish'had a far nicer ring to it than the familiar 'Jimmy Brown' and was a much better option than the daily torments of; "Jimmy Brown went to town,with his knick-ers upside down."

So far as the war was concerned,1942 appeared to be the turn -ing point in terms of optimism and by the end of the year, there was a definite feel and smell of the tide turning in Great Britain's favour. True, the enemy bombers still cont-inued to cause panic but because of the reduced frequency of raids, it was assumed that things were going well for the Allies. Another reason which brought hope to the future of Styal's inmates was the improving supply of movie films that found their way to Styal railway station every Friday. If there was one pleasure more than any other that was unanim-ous amongst the Styal children, it was without doubt the Fri day night pictures. In the winter-time and during the long dark nights,the word 'pictures' was like a beacon shining in the gloom and memories of black and white 'cowboy' and 'car-toon' images radiated hope and laughter and provided a topic of conversation for weeks to come. When thinking about the Friday night pictures,as I had done just a few days before my release, it had dawned on me that going to the pictures was like escaping from the real world and like my hero John Bunyan,all the troublesome worries,problems,and shoulder bur -dens could be dispersed by immersing in the make believe of Utopia. Unfortunately, the reality was that every pleasure had its price and the repetitive words of the home mothers - "no jobs done properly - no pictures'"was an expression used infrequently but rarely instituted. However,there was just one other hiccup to the Friday ritual which prevented anyone from leaving the Home before its execution; pictures or no pictures. Lined-up in single file, the two dozen or more boys assembled in order of seniority and silently awaited their ceremonious fate. How I hated that part of the Friday evening, I thought to myself. I can still picture Miss Ched -ley in her immaculately starched white pinafore followed by her tray carrying assistant as they walked from the kitchen. Starting with the little one's at the begining of the queue, she took a spoon from her breast pocket and poured out some of the contents from the first bottle. Making sure that the whole contents of the spoon had been swallowed, she moved along the line until everyone had received the correct dosage and then returned to the front of the assembly to begin the second dose from another bottle. Only when the third and final dose of medicine had been dished out and Miss Chedley was satisfied that it had been swallowed correctly, was the Home fraternity allowed out to the 'pictures'. To this day the contents of the medicine bottles remains a mystery but as in every routine at Styal,no one reasoned the proceedures and no one dared to refuse an order from authority."I wonder who it was that invented the nicknames for the medicines?; they must have had a good sense of humour." My thoughts of all the hundreds of children going through the same routine down through the years conjured up a comical picture of contorted faces and tortured expressions. The children's interpretation of the white substance from the first bottle was: 'white mickey',a concoction that was totally unbearable to swallow and as tasteless as it was flavourless. Very many times have I tried to interpret the contents of that particular medicine and each time concluded that it was definitely sour milk diluted with water and grated white chalk. Thankfully the taste of the last medicine was the best, and even taken after the dose of cod liver oil its sugary malted flavour helped in eliminating the traces of the previous two.

At ten years of age I began to sense a change in my life. It wasn't a spectacular event nor did it occur on a particular day of the year,but there was a mystic feel about my destiny which suggested a change of direction and purpose. Many's the time during my Styal upbringing that I indulged in a past time of secrecy and privacy, an escapism where fantasy blotted out all my troubles,and tensions became as airborne as the soft overhead cotton-wool clouds. The setting of this beautiful safe haven was the Bollin Valley close to where the river Dean meandered to its rendezvous with the famed Bollin river, a little corner of nature's garden where beams of sunshine danced on the ripples from the stream and inspired my mythical utopia. It was during one of these interludes of tranquility in the not too distant past,whilst equating the why's and wherefore's of one's destiny,that I had a vision of sorts which came about whilst comparing a stone protruding from the river bed. It had the look of a bearded man in old age,much like the Old Father Time and his sickle, and as my gaze wandered over the other stones,it suddenly came to me that the number of stepping stones across the river bed totalled seven. "Seven tens are seventy,the same as the number of years in a man's life; three score years and ten." This muttered observation together with the unusual position of the stones in the water,was enough to convince me that there must be a connection,be it historical or other wise. That,my final thought on the subject,lay dormant until twelve months ago when, once again I found myself perched on the same stretch of river bank,idly paddling my feet in the clear water and gazing nonchalantly at the tiddlers swimming in and out of the dark green strands of moss. It was during that quiet interlude,when the urge to be close to nature over-rided my natural desire to be playing-out with my pals, that a flash of inspiration directed my thoughts and vision to the partly submerged stepping stones on the river bed. In my mind's eye,I looked at the two sides of the river and observed how the water flowed at a much slower pace than the mid stream torrent which,for some reason,reminded me of old age on one side and childhood on the other. Like the nursery house in the orphanage,the shallow water near to the side, offered safety and security before taking the next step into the faster and deeper waters towards mid stream. In short, I visualised in the twinkling of an eye a mental image of the density of water between each of the stones and its comparison to a person's life and concluded that although more dan-gerous, the centre stage of the river held more appeal and more excitement. Before stepping into my sandals ready for the walk up Twinney's Brow,my thoughts lingered for one last time on the river surface and in the sure knowledge that my days at Styal were coming to an end, concluded that my present life in terms of measure, was about two stepping stones from the river bank.

"Brown', Jimmy Brown'" My thoughts had travelled back to a

line-up in the school yard in 1944 when,prior to the commencement of the afternoon session,a prefect had informed me and two other boys that Mr Smith the headmaster wanted us to report to his office before the start of the lessons. Trying my best to put on a brave face,I began my walk down the corridor on legs that felt like lead weights,and my stomach,in reaction to the cold fear,was turning itself upside down. To line up outside the headmasters office meant just one thing, - 'the stick'. Any other punishment in the Homes was nothing compared to the 'stick' off Smiggy (Mr Smith) and even my ritualistic smacking for bed wetting paled into insignificance in comparison. During my past two years as a junior I had occupied the classrooms adjacent to Mr Smith's office and had grown accustomed to observing the line-up of naughty boys and girls awaiting punishment. If I hadn't over heard the screaming and wailing and the shouting and bawling which accompanied every stroke of the cane,then I would have viewed the punishment as a just discipline and not,the awesome nightmare that was now my destiny. The sympathetic look from the boys and girls who were en-route to their classroom was enough to ignite the shivering tremors and in an attempt to divert my concentration somewhere else,I looked at my partners in crime,'Wooksie' and 'Oakbob'. If only we had't found the dead rat during the morning gardening lesson, and if only 'Wooksie' hadn't bent down to catch an escaping frog, then,Miss Flaxton the teacher,wouldn't have caught the full force of gardening soil in her face as I attempted to throw the rat which was on the spade,at 'Oakbob'. "Too late,now,"

I remembered thinking,wondering whether the punishment would consist of three strokes or six strokes.The fear of what lay in store was having such a positive effect on me that my intermittent nervous spasms vied for a joint partnership with my chattering teeth. Finally the office door opened and Smiggy,dressed in his usual brown suit,emerged to administer the response to our naughty prank. "This punishment,for what you did this morning,is going to hurt me more than it will hurt you." As he stood menacingly from his great height,and the sunshine reflecting from his bald head, I tried briefly to interpret the meaning behind his statement. "Let this be a lesson for your future behaviour,and don't let me ever see you in front of my office again." The stick,which until now had been partly concealed under his armpit,was extended to its full length of three or four feet and Wooksie,the first in line,was instructed to hold his arm out to the side of his body. "Higher, higher!" said Smiggy,as he tapped the upturned knuckles. At this point,Wooksie cried out:"Please Sir no'Sir.I won't do it again Sir." His sobs became so infectious that Oakbob and I joined in the crying and glancing at the floor,noticed the puddle where Wooksie had wet himself. "Stop that noise. I haven't started yet." After three more strokes on the other hand,to complete the six strokes,Smiggy said: "When this is finished,you can all mop the floor after you." Through the tears and teeth chattering I was secretly glad that Oakbob was next in line before my turn came.Surely Mr Smith's energy would be depleted before he dealt with me. Finally it was my turn,and again as with Oakbob,he rapped my knuckles to shoulder height to prevent me from withdrawing my hand. According to the school grapevine,if Smiggy raised his right knee when giving the stick,it was an indication of the severity of discipline. Thankfully his feet stayed firm -ly on the wooden corridor floor but this was little consolation for the searing pain on hands that felt as if they were on fire. Looking back on that first encounter with the headmaster was,in a way,my first sensation of mutiny,and the determination to find an alternative to living at Styal became an uppermost priority. Running away,was one option I had considered,but of all the children that did escape,most, if not all,were apprehended and brought back. "There must be a way of getting out of Styal," I remembered thinking at the time. The answer did eventually present itself but not in the way I had imagined.

The summer holidays had come round again,and the prospect of weeks and weeks of playing-out and no more school,at least for a period of time,gave a buoyancy to the rejoicing children. It was during my school vacation,and on one of those balmy summer days that seemed to stand still like a sailing ship waiting for a puff of wind,that I accidently bumped into my sister,Vera. Her long golden hair and pale complexion made her quite distinctive amongst the older group of girls who were busy playing 'rounders', and as I tried to avoid a confrontation with the silly giggling cluster of females,a voice shouted: "Jimmy,Jimmy, I've had a letter." I hadn't seen my sister Vera for some weeks now,apart from a glimpse of her at the Church service and at the parade ground muster.

At this stage of my life girls were an unknown quantity and such was the enforcement of the segregation between the sex-es,any form of contact was liable to yield a bout of shyness. Besides, it was advisable from a boys point of view to avoid being seen with a girl otherwise,the name 'cissy' would att-ache itself to you for a long duration. "Iv'e had a letter from Sylvia," continued Vera as she hustled me to one side. "She's found our Father." Bewildered and bemused at what she was saying,I struggled to find the right words to what sounded like a very complicated issue. "Sylvia says she's go -ing to visit us and bring our Father with her. What do you think of that?" The complexity of it all frightened me and I just wished that I was back with my pals,or better still, alone with my thoughts at the Bollin Valley haven. Somewhere in my subconscious the seeds of Vera's statement had taken root,and sleep that night became interrupted by visions of a white bearded elderly gentleman who was going to take me a-way from Styal. The reality of it all was that I was aware of my Father's age and illness,and I remembered Vera telling me a long time ago that our Dad had been gassed during the first world war and had suffered on and off ever since. The strange thing was, I found myself thinking more and more of the impending visit,and Vera's so-called 'good news', was now a source of optimism responsible for an uplift in spirits. On reflection, it was this news item from Vera together with the main reference to Sylvia's letter which was responsible for an idea concerning my own predicament. Listening to the riverbank orchestra of bird and insect life and feeling more assured by new inspiration,I reflected on the fresh exciting possibility which,by a cross reference to my sister Sylvia, suggested not only a solution to my unhappiness but the answer to my future life. The word; 'scholarship', a simple but meaningful word, was suddenly the discovery of the decade as I consumed the full meaning of its implications. "If I pass my scholarship exams when the time comes,then I'll be free." This thought,and the excitement of this possibility coming true,propelled my thoughts and daydreaming into the realms of fantasy where, in a euphoric state of mind I revelled in a wonderland of family togetherness and freedom. The question of Sylvia's disappearance from the Styal colony had often crossed my inquisitive mind,even to the point of asking myself why, after two years of absence,her transfer had not been made known to me. If Miss Chedley hadn't taken the trouble to explain the prized scholarship that Sylvia had achieved and her consequent move to the Manchester High School,then I would have no doubt carried on presuming that Sylvia had found herself a home and abandoned me and Vera at the orphanage. From now on,I determined, the pursuit of the senior school scholarship was going to be my strategy and,my secret weapon so to speak,which would open the gates to the outside world. After digesting this,my new resolve, I made a promise that nobody,not even Oakbob or Wooksie,would ever know of my intentions.

C H A P T E R   F I V E

"You don't know how lucky you are." How many times had I heard that statement. Usually it was a response from Miss Chedley in retaliation to the dinner left on the plates by some of the children at the end of meal time. Just lately, this same chant had been uttered by the new assistant house-mother,only with more venom and a severe reprimand for any-one caught being wasteful. According to the newly installed Miss McAvoy, there were millions of people in Europe either dying of malnutrition or starving to death,and how their pl-ight was going to be influenced by my portion of food left on my plate,was a complete mystery. "You ungrateful little brat", said Miss McAvoy as she took hold of the plate on wh-ich I had left a combination of Swedes,Turnips and Barley. Clout!, the hairbrush on the side of my head was enough to bring tears to my eyes,but knowing that I would have been sick if I had eaten it,only made me more determined not to. "If you think you have got away with it Brown, then you are mistaken. It will be in front of you at teatime and you wi-ll stay at the table until you have eaten it." Sure enough, I was sick,once I had left the teatime table,but on the plus side of the punishment I discovered from one of the older boys that there was a way of clearing the plate without hav-ing to eat it. Why the idea hadn't occurred to me before now I didn't know. It was so simple. All one had to do was to wait until the housemother's back was turned,and then make a quick swap of plates with whoever liked that particular food, they,would recieve a second helping and I, likewise,would get a kind word of praise for the clean plate. It was obvious that at some stage in the future the house mothers would become wise to the plate swapping exercise and unfortunately it was sooner rather than later that the assistant,Miss McAvoy,became aware of my intense dislike of one particular kind of dish; tripe and cowheel. The very mention of the food let alone the thought of having to eat it,would make me feel sick, and so awesome was the threat of being forced fed that I endured nightmares of the mealtime ritual. It mattered little that there was a choice between eating the tripe and cowheel as a hot stew in a milky sauce or, as a teatime dish served cold,with two slices of bread and butter.So desperate was the situation that I simply had to find an alternative to having to forcibly swallow what felt like tasteless lumps of gristle. The answer,was as uncomplicated as it was elementary. If it wasn't possible to swap plates,then all that one needed to do,was to undo the shirt buttons,then spoon as much dinner down inside the shirt in the quickest time possible. After saying Grace,it was just a simple matter of walking to the outside toilets and emptying the contents of the shirt. "It worked", but for how long,I remembered thinking. The main thing,was the enormous sense of relief at having overcome yet another hurdle.

As much as I hated the thought of having to return to school the summer of 1944 seemed determined in dragging its feet. The news which infiltrated the Styal Homes concerning the seemingly far off war,appeared to improve with every week and one sensed that only a matter of months separated the return of normality to a country village already prepared for the transition to post-war tranquility. In my opinion,Styal would always portray the sleepy village nestling alongside the Bollin Valley and just as it had awoken to the calling of wartime activities,so too would it don nature's seasonal mantle before returning to hibernation.

"I wish it was this time next year, I might be living in the city of Manchester and riding on trams, preferably alongside the driver or even on the top deck." Thinking out loud, my imagination traced the exciting journeys ahead and the fascinating patterns of tram lines and overhead point systems.

"I wish I could pass all my exams before next summer and then I might qualify for the scholarship which will take me away from Styal." Wish upon wish seemed to dominate my fantasies as my aspirations increased with age,and my dreams, the driving force behind my future, mapped out my stairway to my impending destiny. Now the war was nearing its ending there was a noticeable influx of visitors arriving for the Saturday visiting period when, on arrival at the gates, they were required to sign in at the Lodge Home. Observing this weekend proceedure from my outpost -a den inside the hedgerow outside the Church- I became fascinated by the bag-carrying individuals who sat on the wooden bench in front of the Lodge and who,at intervals, would produce sweets and other produce from bags and brown paper parcels. Sometimes,the visitors would bring comics and books and I would make a mental note of the boys who received them,so that at a later date I could ask to borrow them or make a trade with sweets or anything else I had worth swapping. "One day,I will have a visit from my sister Sylvia,and hopefully she will bring me lots of sweets and comics and take me and Vera out of the Homes for a while." Continuing this line of thought,I listed in my mind all my favourite titles,including the Hotspur, the Beano,and the Dandy.

The number 64 bus came to a sudden halt at the junction of a cross road leading to the city and momentarily,my thoughts came to an abrupt ending. The roads leading to Manchester were becoming wider and busier by the mile but as yet,there were no signs of any trams. "Only a matter of a short distance," I concluded, "and probably,there'll be plenty of them, all converging on the inward route to town." Like the weather,my enthusiasm which had begun with the exciting journey ahead,had now lost some of its initial sparkle,and the golden sunshine of early morning had been replaced by a misty haze,which to my mind resembled a jaundiced yellowy colour. My birds-eye view from the bus was now projecting a strange world of comings and goings where busy people travelling in all directions and all seemingly with a sense of purpose were committing their daylight hours to a dedicated mission. This scene below me reminded me of a similar comparison that had been witnessed from a wooded den overlooking the river Dean and from somewhere in my mind's recess I recalled the moment when,after a punishment of strokes from a slipper,I had retreated to my Styal hideaway. At the time,and after the usual thoughts of escape had subsided,there was an interlude of mental blankness and it was then,whilst staring at the ground in front of me that one of my inspirational urges conjured up a picture illustrating a part of life hitherto without meaning. Intensifying my stare at the hundreds of tiny ants in front of me I suddenly identified with the uniform antics of a species of nature who's antics bore an uncanny resemblance to the situation concerning the children of the Styal Homes. The comparison was astonishing. In front of me lay an ants nest,a colony,where all the residents adhered to a timetable of working patterns essential to the success and survival of the outpost. Observing the ants as they criss-crossed in columns was like looking down on the Styal Homes colony,with sections of children marching here and there attending their specified jobs of work and generally obeying orders from within the chain of command. I had heard Miss Chedley on occasions,refer to the Home's work rotas as being the mark of "good husbandry" and although there was a vagueness about its meaning I assumed the interpretation to be something to do with keeping the house in order, much like the ants, productive, busy,and always attending a job of work of some description.

The country sights and sounds that had been a major part of my life were now disappearing in the wake of the Manchester bound bus. Gone now,was the quiet landscape which had greeted every dawning of my childhood and with it,a sadness that was begining to creep over me with every realization that it had gone forever. Reflecting on this and many other aspects of Styal,I was suddenly conscious of the fact that my rural home was not quite the hushed landscape projected in my mind and my reflections on the orchestral sounds of nature in a setting of woodland close to the orphanage could only dwell on one particular culprit of the noisy ensemble; the crow. Their constant cawing,begining with the frenzied springtime chorus and ending with the lethargic wintertime intermission was so much a part of the Styal scene that their exclusion from the landscape would have made the stage performance incomplete. In many ways,their's was a tragic story,and sadly to say,one which would always bring to mind the cruelties in -flicted on a harmless species of nature by human beings. The word 'verminous', as used by the Boss,had little significance,probably because the meaning of the word fell on deaf ears,but when he spoke of the crow as being the number one enemy of the farmers and farmland,it became interpreted as a green light for the crow's wanton death and destruction. This,was my own view, and maybe it was my feeling of guilt at having been involved in the injustice meted out to the crows,that was prompting me to look around for some excuse. "It was only natural", I told myself, all the boys did it; the younger one's used sticks and stones and slings,whilst the older mature lads plied their skills with catapaults. Thinking back to that period,I could remember my first 'crow shoot' encounter and especially, one of its casualties as it hopped on one leg through the undergrowth of the Styal Woods, its wings flapping like broken sails and terror written in its eyes. The sound of gunfire one Saturday afternoon was enough to arouse a curious excitement,and joining the group of boys headed for the woods,I overheard the comments:"Boss is shooting crows". This sanctioning of what appeared to be an extermination of wildlife was, so far as the crows were concerned, their death warrant. If the Superintendant wasn't shooting them, then it would probably be 'us lads' stoning or catapaulting them to death with well aimed sling shot. Some of the home mothers would make crow pie from the blood-ied corpses but thankfully,Miss Chedley preferred not to. If there was one memory that could be eliminated from my mind it would be the one which depicted the crows spiralling down through the tree branches prior to the bludgeoning blows and the final coup-de-grace delivered unmercifully.

With a hurried retreat from this depressing line of thought I once again elected the Dean Valley as the more cheering prospect where, along with my pals Wooksie and Oakbob,I pad-dled upstream under a clear blue sky. In the far distance I could see the viaduct which carried the rail link between Wilmslow and Styal and beyond the arches on the other side of Stanneylands lay the fruit orchard,the one reputed as ha-ving the best apples in Styal. Above the hillside to the left,the rooftop of the Homes hospital was just visible,and on the opposite side,some distance from the river,lay Lacey Green,a suburb of Wilmslow. If ever the winter was severe e-nough,this very spot between the Homes and Stanneylands Road became the ideal location for the best tobogganing run in Styal and when thinking about the good times,my flashes of memory would usually locate on the hillside where a homemade toboggan would be transporting me towards a swollen river. It was strange how I found myself a part of this trio,glanc-ing at the two pals in front of me. None of us were alike, and yet we each seemed to compliment each other, much like the blind leading the blind. Wooksie,was about my age and slightly taller,and because of a nervous disorder would some times speak with an impediment. He had often been the object of ridicule by the other boys and much to my sorrow,had in-curred the wrath of the teachers for not sounding his words correctly. Because of his inability to roll his tongue ar-ound the letter 'R', he would more often than not use the letter 'W',which not only altered the 'ragged rascal' to the 'wagged wascal' but caused the other children to laugh all the more at his affliction. The name 'Wooksie' had been born from yet another mispronunciation and who the author of this, his nickname was, will always remain a mystery. However, the name Wooksie, was a title used only by his closest friends, whereas by the rank and file of the colony, he was subjected to the harmless taunts of 'Wooks and Cwose', an inscription which demonstrated his failings to pronounce the correct syl -lables to Rooks and Crows. Oakbob,on the other hand, was as normal as any of the other Styal children except,for one failing, his height. He appeared to be a good ten inches sm -aller than anyone else around his age and his personality, unaffected by the name calling or any other reference to his stature, made him a popular figure throughout the Homes. In his own words, Oakbob had once told me of how he inherited his nickname, a revelation that always brought a smile to my face. "We were digging a ditch in the potatoe field near to the school in readiness for the foundations of the emergency air raid shelter. The other class-mates had already climbed out of the trench in readiness for some kind of inspection by the Boss,but when I attempted to make my way up the newly dug embankment,it caved in. By the time my shouts had been heard,the Superintendant had arrived,and walking over to the excavation he looked down and said: "you look just like an oakbob waiting to take root." Maybe,it was Oakbob's lack of height which caused him to be more studious than most of the other boys and instead of a physical involvement on the play -ing field, he was more often than not inside the pages of a book. Being a pal of Oakbob had its rewards,in that he had a mother on the outside who regularly sent him comics and if it hadn't been for his generous nature,my sources of inspiration for my own wishing world would have been destitute.

As much as I disliked the boring routine of church religious worship, Eastertime in the colony always projected an annual upsurge in righteousness. The culmination of weeks of Sunday School preparation ended with a mass display of celebration uniting everyone in the church; from the youngest tots under supervision,to the older boys and girls,and finally the Home Mothers. Only two other events had the effect of drawing me closer to the church,one being the Christmas celebration,for obvious reasons,and the other,the Harvest Festival. All of the three were inspiring in their own way but I distinctly remember my close feelings of affinity with anything which was associated with Easter. Easter Sunday began as always with the distribution of a hard boiled egg at breakfast-time and accompanying the spoon on the plate was also a black col -oured crayon. This was the only day of the year,apart from

Christmas,when routine became relaxed and instead of eating on command and observing the sacred mealtime silence,a mild mayhem took over,and with it a display of artistic abandonment. Face drawing on the outer shell was always encouraged by Miss Chedley and when in her opinion the egg bearing the best likeness had been selected,the recipient received a shiny new penny. Maybe it was this light hearted interlude at the begining of the day that spilled over into the morning Church service,and what with all the radiance from the Easter hymns and Easter music,the momentum of good feeling seemed to last the whole day. Analysing my thoughts on this topic and thinking back to all the past Eastertimes,my conclusion was,as always,linked to a one syllable word, 'hope', a word which,during my latter years at Styal,had been the driving force in my ever optimistic search for a future beyond the perimeter gates of the colony. Following the recent winter of dull routines and grey skies hope,lay in the brigh-tness of the sunbeams filtering throught the coloured skylights of the Church windows suggesting that springtime had at last arrived and with it,the anticipated awakening of natures wonderland. Through the warming rays another hope became rekindled as I contemplated the year ahead of me and, the all important scholarship. This,was the year when my one hope above all others could come to fruition and my boyhood dream a reality.

In terms of history,the German surrender and the monumental British victory in early May of 1945 will forever be etched in the chronicles of the nation,as will the memory of the ensuing peace celebrations throughout the world. In my minds diary, the events affiliated to the end of war festivities in May were in some ways the prelude to a new era in my life as new and exciting forces mingled with my fantasies of the future. In my whole life, I had never before witnessed a real bonfire, and the stories that circulated in the colony with regard to Guy Fawkes and Bonfire night were, due to the war, still mythical. On the second Saturday in May the celebrations grew to a fever pitch as preparations got under way for what was termed as the biggest bonfire Styal had ever seen. For fear of setting the trees alight adjacent to the offices and parade ground, the site had been located on the football field near to the main road, a more suitable position in terms of spectator participation and accommodation. "M'm, there's a bonfire on Gerald Grady's bed." Recalling the exciting moments of that night when portions of treacle toffee had been consumed in close proximity to the raging inferno, I couldn't resist the smile which brought back to mind the mid night episode of that same evening. Waking up suddenly, and sitting upright, I saw a fire on the bed opposite to mine, and in panic and concern for the sleeping occupant I raced along the corridor to the house mother's bedroom. Within moments of my continuous knocking she peered round the doorway in a dressing gown, her facial expressions questioning the rude interruptions to her night's sleep. "M'm, come quick, there's a fire on Gerald Grady's bed." I can't quite remember how I was coaxed back to my bed nor, how the fire was extinguished but come the next day, after an examination of the burning bed linen I concluded that the whole incident had been a vivid nightmare,an apparition due to my accute sense of emotional excitement. The school term between Easter and Summer became more demanding as the weeks rolled on towards the holiday season,and for those girls and boys like myself,studying for a scholarship,every lesson in the classroom seemed to necessitate more concentration than ever. In terms of anxiety,I didn't know which was worse, the actual exams or the waiting for the final result. Eventually just two weeks before the summer term,whilst attending the morning assembly, an announcement was made by Smiggy concerning the winners of the scholarships. "This year,has seen a high standard of work from all the contestants,and it is a credit to the Styal Senior School and its teachers that no less than seven pupils have attained the necessary qualification marks." Proceeding with his oratory he continued; "It is with great satisfaction that I now announce the names of the winners of the scholarships and,the name of the school they will be removing to next term." All the names of the boys and girls were announced individually and each one received a handclap from the school audience in recognition of their success. By the time the sixth name had been called I had become resigned to the fact that I had squandered my one remaining hope of leaving the Homes colony. Defeat was staring me in the face and just as I began contemplating the life sentence ahead of me,my name reverberated from the four walls with a deafening crescendo. "James Brown. Yew Tree Secondary School." The applause became lost in the background as I tried to grasp the reality of the situation. "I've done it, I've done it." This exclamation,repeated at regular intervals under my breath,became my password for the rest of the day as I proudly basked in the glory of my achievement. Reviewing this very poignant moment in my life,I remember going to bed that night after telling Miss Chedley my good news and remembering how I had previously prayed for my dreams to come true,I knelt at the side of the bed with clasped hands and thanked Jesus for all his help. Quickly jumping into bed be-fore any of my pals noticed my religious trait,I gazed for what seemed an eternity as dusk became darkness,my mind torn between excitement and surrender. "I wonder if I will be able to ride on a tram to school?" "I wonder where I will live?" "I wonder if I will see my sister Sylvia?" "I wonder what the new school will be like?" All of these questions seemed to multiply as the days became weeks and at one stage I even considered making an approach to my sister Vera. By nature I could worry about the slightest thing and my sensitivity could induce doubts for no apparent reason,but somewhere at the back of my mind my intuition was informing me of something that wasn't quite adding up properly. "There must be a reason for the delay with my scholarship transfer. Maybe they can't find a home for me at the moment and that will mean travelling on a bus every day to the new school." Faced with the prospect of jumping from one conclusion to an-other,I decided there and then that I would put all thought to one side and concentrate on the remaining weeks of the summer holidays.

Come the last Sunday before the new school term,when the children were preparing their minds for the transition to an Autumn curriculum, I remembered thinking that my own particular involvement was almost at an end and that any contribution on my part was merely temporary. The mid-day Sunday walk which took place the week preceeding the return to School,was yet another reminder that not only could this be my last view of the Carrs Woods but a possible final farewell to the beautiful picturesque valley of my childhood. Walking under the overhead archway of shaded tree branches down the notorious Twinney's Brow,the home mother had indicated that in return for good behaviour,she would consent to a leisurely stroll around the lake at Lindow Common where she could gather some of her favourite Yellow Broom. Preoccupied with thoughts of an uncertain future ahead, added an extra dimension to the day's events,and every now and then,a touch of sadness accompanied the warm splinters of sunlight falling from above. "If this was to be my last memory of Styal" I remember thinking, "then let it be commemorated to the woods and landscape of the Bollin Valley." Crossing the Dean river in crocodile formation I glanced at the bomb crater and the meadow leading to the Styal Woods,aware that the fragrant carpet of bluebells had vacated their hillside many weeks ago. The Bluebell Woods of Styal was a landmark known to all the Homes children and villagers alike,as was the ancient stone monument of the Boddington dynasty who's crumbling remains perched precariously in the Carrs,never failed to destract exploration en-route to Lindow Common. Tracing the winding river through the Carrs on the return journey, I would have given anything to have been able to shed my Sunday suit of clothes in exchange for just a pair of shorts, and then, just to be able to paddle down stream to the humpback bridge. The bend of the river where the exposed cliff of red sandstone compelled exploration, was another of my favourite haunts and only during the past year, along with my pals, had I discovered the ultimate pleasure from climbing the cliff face and then sliding down its slippery surface to the river below. Wartime, and the effects of war, had in the main, gone unnoticed in the Styal village whereas in Wilmslow, the Bollin Valley and the grassy verges of the Carrs, had become an off duty playground for the scores of military personnel who were stationed in and around the vicinity. Looking back to a day sometime before my anticipated departure, I remembered coming face to face with the many pairs of blue uniformed men and women who, in their RAF and WAAF costumes, appeared to line the whole length of the river bank at intervals of every few yards. In total innocence and with an ignorance as yet of boy and girl chemistry, I concluded that the uniformed males were simply holding hands with their partners in a gesture of farewell before departure to their overseas destination. In later years there would be more than ample proof that the hand-holding between couples was a mere preliminary in the various stages of courtship and, that the obvious finale would manifest itself in the unusual plague of small white balloons dotted along the banks of the Bollin.

C H A P T E R   S I X

Monday morning, the new Autumn term, and the clockwork begin -ings of yet another chapter in the day to day function of Styal Homes, was signalled by the familiarity of the buglar boy. His rendering of the 'revellie' at 8-30,became the signal for the wheels of industry to begin turning but more to the point,reminded the children on parade that holidays were now at an end and only the strict rules of discipline would be tolerated. Marching to school that morning with an air of indifference to what lay ahead,my confidence albeit,a lit -tle uncertain, I still retained the belief that today, all the information regarding my scholarship would be made known. After the assembly,and the solemnities which failed to make reference to my dilemma, I hesitantly lined up amongst the pupils of the new class in which I has been included. "Jimmy Brown, you've got to report to the headmaster's office and wait outside." Thoughts of the stick started an immediate chain reaction but before my nerves got the better of me I assured myself that this visit was merely an interview about my new school and not,the punishment ritual synonymous with the normal summons. Watching the Shakespear House prefect disappear in to the classroom and myself isolated from the new term introductions, I concluded that my presence at the headmaster's door added up to what could only be the begining of a new future. From my vantage point,even with my eyes trained ahead of me,I could tell by the echoing footsteps th -at Mr Smith's presence was imminent and again I reassured myself that this was not a punishment appointment. During my short time at the senior school I had become very familiar with two of Smiggy's major habits and even through my closed eyelids I could picture him digging around inside his ears with a girls hairgrip and then holding the instument up high whilst he inspected the rewards of his labours. Not quite so repulsive but still obvious from any distance,was his contin -uous manner of scratching his backside through the coarse fabric of his suit and his identity so far as I was concern-ed revolved around these two distinguished practices. Having closed the door behind his entrance to his private sanctum, another few minutes elapsed before the command was issued to enter. "Come in, Brown." Closing the door behind me and trying not to let the magnitude of the importance show in my temperament,I stood to attention in readiness of his announc -ement. "Jimmy Brown." At this point of the proceedure and before another word was uttered I knew there was not going to be a scholarship. It was the quiet,almost gentle tone of voice which, coupled with the fact that for the first time in my life he had called me by my first name, suggested that what he was about to disclose was perhaps more in the way of an apology. Continuing the conversation he went on; "I'm afraid I have some bad news for you. Due to a miscalculation by the examiners your marks were wrongly placed and because of this reason you will not now be eligible to leave Styal Senior School on a scholarship."

Looking back on this episode as one of my saddest and unjust experiences of my life, I have repeatedly asked the question, why me. Why was it that my marks were wrongly added and not anybody else's. And, more importantly, why wasn't I allowed another chance to sit the examination again. Unfortunately, these and many other questions became a negative response to the obvious answer and in retrospect I was grateful that Mr. Smith had spared me the embarrassing mention of bed-wetting. Walking from the interview to my new classroom I felt the weight of depression like a black cloud across my shoulders and with a renewed hatred and resentment of the system that had robbed me of my one chance, I resolved to devise a plan of action that would enable me to escape from Styal. A few weeks on and with all thoughts of an Autumn escape momentarily suspended, my world in the institution had taken on a whole new dimension. I was now classed as an 'older' boy, a title which carried the burden of more responsibilities and one which meant that for the next two years at least, I would always be eligible for any job of work in the Home. Apart from the usual mundane jobs of work affiliated to the dining and kitchen areas, 'us' senior boys also took on the more demanding and strenuous duties as defined in a weekly rota. Alternating between weeks on and weeks off, the jobs, all of them varying according to the season, were on completion, subject to a thorough inspection by the home mother who either 'passed' them or rejected them as being in need of another attempt. Some of the jobs such as dusting, sweeping, window cleaning, polishing floors and furniture, potato peeling, boot and shoe cleaning, chopping firewood, and many more more mundane assignments grew so familiar and routinely boring that in the end, they became a drudgery. One chore designated to the older boys was the one itemized as 'flu cleaning and fire lighting' and although this required an early start of 6.30 in the morning,the reward on completion made the effort all the worth while. The first stage after a silent shivering descent down the stairs was to cover the kitchen floor and work-tops with dust sheets. From now,the whole operation be -came a race against time in order to provide the essential heat and hot water for breakfast and for the rest of the day To bring the big kitchen range (ovens) back to life required a well ordered routine and precision with every proceedure. Once the soot and clinkers had been scraped out of the grate and the flu's emptied of their ashes,it was time to move on to the next stage. Resembling a chimney sweep,it was now a testing time to see if combustion would escalate all the pre parations such as having rolled the paper into tight enough balls and having laid the small kindling wood at just the right pressure and angle. Providing the wood was dry enough to catch and hold on to the flame,then it was just a matter of waiting for the right moment in which to place the lumps of coal onto the glowing embers Presuming success had taken place and the roar of the fire was producing the right total of heat and velocity,then it was time for the fully filled kettle to be placed on the heated surface. During the period which allowed for the water to come to the boil and before the ovens became to hot,it was time for the polishing and black-leading of all the handles and surfaces of the kitchen range,a task which concluded the morning's work schedule. Before clearing up the aftermath,and making sure of the temp -erature of the surface of the stove, one remaining task was to stir the large pan of porridge made the night before by the Home mother and then place it to warm on the outside per-imeter of the hob. Now, after a wash and tidy, it was my reward time in which the housemother after an inspection, invited me to sit in front of the warm fire whilst she served up a mug of hot cocoa and two slices of bread and dripping.

"Would you like to join the Church choir?" This out of the blue question by the Boss, some weeks before Christmas was an-swered with an emphatic 'yes' in a response which needed no second thoughts. I had heard from my pal Wooksie that being in the choir was "tons better than sitting in the Church pew and being watched constantly by the housemother" and, more re-warding still, he had said, "the choir go on an outing every year." Just lately, the church services were begining to cast long shadows of confinement during an hour long service that seemed more like a two hour marathon of fidgeting and "wait till I get you home" threats. No sooner had I passed the singing test devised by the choir master when again out of the blue, I was approached by Mr Dillion of the Styal Band who, having heard that I had an ear for music, offered to enrol me as a bandboy. Having been accepted into the Styal Homes Military Band not only boosted my morale but promoted a whole string of possibilities including, being excused duties in the Home, due to band practice. When asked to choose an instrument of my choice, I decided on the euphonium, a decision which came after trying out the array of big polished bass instruments. There was something about the euphonium which felt snug and comfortable, and along with the equally satisfying feel of the mouthpiece and hand grip,I knew I had made the right selection. The upstairs Bandroom which lay directly adjacent to the stables in the cobbled work yard be came like a second home to me,and for the next two years,the musical echo's of 'Blaze Away', 'Colonel Bogey' and 'Unter Den Dopple Adler', were to become haunting melodies due to the hours and hours of practice,practice,and more practise. Hitting the wrong notes,or any other misdemeanour,was reward -ed with having to clean the bandroom and scrub the splinter strewn wooden floors,a task which as usual,was performed on a Saturday afternoon. In terms of social standing,being a band boy was a step on the eletist ladder and whenever work-ing gangs were required,band commitments would always super-sede the argument. According to the array of polished cups and shields bearing the insignia of the Styal Homes Military Band,it was obvious that the Band was steeped in a military background,a fact which was evident through the continuous parading and marching in and around the colony. The comical figure of Oakbob brought a smile to my face as I pictured a small boy covered in a protective leopardskin outfit,support -ing a huge bass drum and flanked on either side by his tall associates. His talent on the drums was acknowledged by all the band members both at band practice and on the stage when performing in the numerous band engagements. Like myself,he couldn't read a note of music, and I remembered thinking at the time he had divulged this information that drummers had the easiest job in the band and therefore didn't need music like the other instumentalists. Looking back,I have often marvelled at my own survival as a band boy and although I be came very proficient as a musician, my one secret dread was in having to sit a written exam, a task which I knew, would have spelled failure. Fortunately,Mr.Dillion left the Homes before my exam requirements became due and since the Band-master's position remained unfilled,my secret remained safe.

Christmas Day, especially the one following the war's ending seemed to have a feel of excitement more than the previous Christmases. Maybe it was being in the band and playing in my first stage concert which promoted a stirring feeling of optimism about my future prospects in the year ahead. On the other hand,maybe it was the thought of all those jellies and cakes etc., which had been put aside as a reward for the Christmas musical programme. The usual Christmas stocking left on my bed that morning had contained an extra item,and instead of the normal marbles and a comic, Father Christmas had added an orange. However,the real and most pleasurable part of Christmas Day began at 11-30, when, after a short morning church service, the entire child population of Styal Homes queued excitedly inside the recreation hall in expectation of being given the main Christmas present by a Father Christmas. On arrival at the Christmas tree and,the bulging table bearing all the gifts,the children's patience was rewarded with their name being called out and, the subsequent package handed to them by Father Christmas. Opening my gift parcel,and revealing what the Manchester Town Hall had sent me this year, I was delighted with the toy glider airplane made from balsa wood and matching kit with RAF insignia and, the appropiate elastic catapault necessary for the lift off. All too soon the partying came to a close,but before the final curtain came down on the festivities,one remaining treat,the ultimate in terms of entertainment,lay in wait for the eager children of the colony, - the visit to the famous Belle Vue Circus in Manchester. The fever of anticipation in connection with the circus and the impending ride on a bus from Styal,provoked such an enthusiasm that the children's exuberance threatened to burst open the gates of the Homes.

"Jimmy Brown!" A girls voice called out my name and then re peated it over and over. "Jimmy Brown, Matron wants to see you at the office." Leaving my pals to continue the game we had been playing,I hurried through the workyard to the Super -intendant's quarters,a puzzled expression exposing my anx- iety over what misdemeanor I might have committed. Answering my knock,the Matron took my hand and led me into the office where Mrs Huggins the Superintendant's wife was seated be- hind the desk. "Well!, Jimmy Brown, I don't know what we're going to do with you," she said,in an unusually apologetic tone of voice. "Matron informs me that there are not enough seats to go round for the circus trip and therefore,we have decided to send only the best behaved children. You will get another chance next year." Staring in disbelief at the wall in front of me and mentally refusing to accept what she was trying to tell me,I became totally inattentive and blanked out my mind under the descending clouds of despondency. "Did you hear what I said? Why dont you really try to stop your bed wetting. Answer me." "Yis M'm," I replied, in a stuporous and defeatist attitude. Signalling to Matron that the interview was ended she concluded; "off you go then, Jimmy Brown, and remember what I've asked you to do, try harder." My first reaction on leaving the office was to run down the sloping pathway to the woods, seeking sanctuary in the only way I knew, that of being alone in my secret world where all the elements of nature offered a safe haven from adversities. Unfortunately it was still wintertime and the coldness from being too close to the river bank only intensified my spate of shivering. With glistening teardrops begining to blur my vision, I made a retreat through the cobbled square in the direction of the stables where, from a recent discovery, I had found a hiding place amongst the empty pens. Huddled in the warming bales of straw, I settled down to evaluate once more, my future at the orphanage, and again I concluded that escape from this prison, was the only option left. "I know, I'll wait until the warmer weather comes after Easter." Looking back to that moment, a time when thoughts became mountainous, and wishing, confused with reality, a chink of light settled on one particular line of thought. The effect was like having made an important discovery. "Why hadn't I realised the fact before now. There were others in the Homes who shared the same misery as me." By accepting this new development I renewed my sense of vision and with a clearing-out of debris from my mind, I rescued my sinking spirit by putting things into a new perspective. Only recently, a new code of rules regarding discipline had been introduced inside the colony and 'good hidings' were becoming a thing of the past,which, if you wet the bed,was very good news indeed. However, this new and seemingly safer alternative proved in my case, to be fraught with sinister physcological trauma, and a return to physical punishment emerged as the more desirable of the two. Carrying a bundle of sheets to the laundry was,in itself, a normal function in the day to day routine, except,that is,at 8.30am,just before the bugle call for school. At that time of the day,the only other boys and girls performing this see -mingly innocent duty were the ones who had the same impediment as me. Funny,how I had overlooked this obvious conclusion,that there were others in this same predicament,and yet, because of the very personal stigma attached to this early morning assignment,the task of taking one's washing to the laundry,was performed by faceless people who, like me,hugged the hedgerows to avoid eye contact or recognition. This,was the very reason I concluded,that receiving punishment in the Home was a far better preference. At least,the secret stayed within the four walls whereas now,my privacy was subject to varying degrees of humiliation and increased levels of anxiety.

Styal Woods, the playground to many countless hundreds of children over many generations,held a particular appeal to the male population of the Homes especially,in Springtime and Summertime. These,were the seasons when the older boys who,having finished their work schedules,would descend on an area of the woods near to the stables and indulge in their favourite pastime, - tobogganing.

The tobaggan run had been accidently created by the boiler-house engineer,Mr Mottershead,who,over a long period of time had used the embankment for tipping ashes and clinkers from his ovens,thus establishing a ready made surface for summer-time sledging. Unconventional and clumsy,the toboggans,made from discarded sheets of corrugated metal roofing,became transformed into chariots of human projectiles with a seating capacity of up to eight persons. The most successful chariot was the one which not only had a highly polished surface and undercarriage and curved-up front structure,but also carried a proficient driver who could steer the contraption down the uneven course without colliding with tree stumps or other major obstacles. "Jimmy Brown!" This address by the home-mother in a raised tone of voice was the reaction to the sight which met her eyes as I limped into the kitchen. "What on earth have you done to yourself?" "I fell off the back of the toboggan M'm," was the reply I gave, screwing my face up in agony. "You'll have to go the hospital at once" said Miss Chedley as she surveyed the remnants of my trousers and the bloodied pulp of flesh which had previously been my back-side. Limping along Church avenue,supported by two older boys,I finally arrived at the hospital infirmary and was immediately ordered to lie face down on the wooden bench. For the next half hour or so,through reactive "oogh's and argh's" I had enough time to ponder at my foolishness,when I had insisted on jumping on the back of the overladen toboggan and ended up half on and half off. The application of the hyper-dermic needle and the subsequent administering to the wound produced a curt "don't be such a cry baby" as I screamed out in agony at every contact to my sensitive anatomy. "You'll have to stay in hospital for a few days" said Sister,as she handed me a tumbler of medicine to drink. Signalling to the nurse that the surgery was finished ,the white uniformed Sis -ter gave her instructions about my removal to a ward at the far end of the corridor. Turning to help in the adjustments for my assisted walk to the dormitory,she pointed her finger and said:"and don't you get out of bed until you're told to"

Time and time again and for various reasons, I have looked back on my hospitalisation as a major milestone in my life. The hospital, a single storey building situated on the outer perimeters of the institution,was familiar to the residents of the colony for one very ominous reason,-the dentist. However,now that I was viewing my confinement from the inside so to speak,it's antiseptic interior presented a pictue of unbelievable contrast to anything I had ever known. Gone, momentarily,was the familiar drab habitation,where home was a bedroom containing eight iron bedsteads,an open fireplace flanked by four bare walls,and a window space covered in a matching set of dark green window blinds. Trying my best to ignore the pain and discomfort,my eyes became focused on my new surroundings,a room which apart from its beautiful appearance,projected a true image of what I imagined a real home would look like. The curtains and bedside screens both included the same delicately coloured patterns and were the main feature to a highly polished floor space containing six white bedsteads and two baby cots. All around me,including the walls and ceiling,the same bright outlook became mirrored in a panorama of fantasy and bewilderment, and just as if somebody had added the finishing touch, the scenario became complete with the large vase of flowers standing solitary on the centre table. Warmed by the warm sunshine that had penetrated the windows for most of the day,the hospital ward be-came akin to a very familiar bible quotation,and all of a sudden,I surrendered my anxieties and "lay my head to rest". Yielding to the powerful forces of sleep and drugs, I capitulated to the influence of all that had occurred that afternoon and instead of seeking my usual sleep of escapism,I dis-covered for the first time in my life an alternative slumber when,having been tucked in by the nurse,I succumbed to a sleep of contentment and sanctuary. "I wish I could stay in hospital", became my first reaction in a new spate of wishes from my luxurious surroundings. I had noticed that only two other children were resident in the ward but unfortunately they were too young and too ill to form any sort of communicative relationship. Instead, after my dressings had been changed,the bed remade,and the breakfast tray cleared, I was instructed by the nurse to lie on my stomach and help myself to the supply of comics in the cupboard of the bedside cabinet. I couldn't believe my luck. A whole bundle of comics to myself and all the time in the world in which to read my favourite cartoons. "I wish we had bedside lockers in the Homes,then I could keep my marbles and comics locked up instead of hiding them in secret hiding places." Before being tucked up for the night,the nurse informed me that because I was making good progress in my healing recovery,it probably wouldn't be necessary to stay in hospital any longer than an -other day. "If that was the case,then tomorrow I'll read all the comics I can find." This, my final thought for the day,soon became forgotten as my restless mind turned towards the Home and the question of what my pals had been doing in my absence. Whilst there was a willingness to wallow in my new circumstances and defect from my work routines for as long as possible, there was also a growing unrest which suggested that I rejoin my pals as soon as possible,in the continual quest for new adventure. Gazing at the curtains and silhouetting the designs through half closed eyelids,another day became another night,and the glow from the blue dimmer lights projected a galaxy of eerie shadows across the room where white robed sentinels stood as angels along the milky way. Some time later,in the midst of that same evening, I returned to my surroundings to find a real-life angel standing by my bedside wearing a nightgown,and when I asked why she had woken me from my slumber,she replied; "I've come to visit you from my bed in the isolation ward." Older and taller than me,she ordered me to make room in the bed for her and in the same whispered tone of voice,told me not to say anything to anybody,especially Sister. "Lie on your back," she continued, and ignoring the painful re-positioning of my wounded posterior,I responded with an eagerness that belied any thought of guilt or timidness. Her next move was to sit across my upper thighs and having found a comfortable position,lifted her nightdress to expose a part of Mother Nature that was totally alien to me. My shyness,like my inquisitiveness,was becoming more apparent as she continued to fumble with my bits and pieces until at last, she appeared to have succeeded in connecting our bodies together. I remembered thinking to myself how innocent I was in terms of knowledge and experience in matters concerning girls and especially of the sexual act. My understanding of such things was a hundred per cent nil except perhaps with one exception,the bulls and cows of Park's Farm,who's antics in mounting the opposite sex, always attracted prolonged stares from the passing school formations. Whether the female night intruder gained a positive satisfaction from her gyrations can only be guessed at,whereas my own reaction of rythmic 'oogh's' and 'aagh's' came not from any sense of fulfilment,but from the agonising punishment to my backside. Sensing that my responses were inspired by my medical affliction,she dismounted and placed a wet kiss on my lips before making a swift exit. Wiping the kiss from my face,I quickly turned on my side to relieve the soreness, and reflecting on my uninvited guest who,in her sinful abuse of my privacy had exposed my immaturity, I concluded that this was one experience that would be treasured for many months to come. When sleep finally took over,it was a conundrum of excitement and pleasure, uniting the sexual boundaries and the sweet taste of forbidden fruit. "You wont be going home today," were the words of the early morning nurse as she surveyed the bloodied sheets. "You look as if you were on that toboggan again,last night." Nodding my head in agreement, I conceded that I did indeed feel very sore. "You really must,lie on your stomach when you go to sleep,otherwise you'll never get better." "Yis M'm," was my quick reply. For one brief moment my day dreaming eclipsed the seriousness side of what Nurse was was trying to tell me and in the blink of an eyelid,I captured the ghostly figure of the angel wearing the white nightgown. Smiling inwardly, I reassured myself of the reality of the previous night and vowed there and then that this special secret, my only possession,would by mine to savour for the rest of my life. Like everything else at Styal.the good times only had short lives and my elation of the past thirty six hours became a shattered memory in the wake of a major new discovery. Perhaps I should have stayed on my bed like I was told. The trouble was, I had read all the available comics and boredom was begining to set in. If only the doctor and his nursing staff hadn't been called to a patient on another ward. It wasn't like me to be nosy,and to defy authority was equally alien to my nature,but on seeing the abandoned trolley near to my bed with its contents of important looking documents,the temptation became too much of a challenge. A swift glance at the top folder revealed my personal details: JAMES ARTHUR BROWN - NUT COTTAGE. Trying my best to ignore the gnawing guilt symptoms and the rapid increase in heartbeats,I placed a comic over the top of the file and quickly turned the page. Two or three of the words such as; disability, symptom, and another now forgotten,were instantly recognisable,but when it came to the long scribbled word following the bold heading: "ILLNESS",my gaze became riveted to a jumble of letters spelling out my debility. Replacing the folder as quickly as possible, I climbed onto the bed and adopted my normal lying position,fixing my stare on the blank wall space between the upright bed posts. I had never heard of this disease before but it was evident that all knowledge of my infirmity was be-ing kept from me. In a mild panic,and under threat from an increasing state of grievance,I tried to pronounce the word which spelled doom to my immediate future. From the evidence shown in black and white,it was obviously 'Noctersesis', or, then again,it could be 'Nocteresis', but which ever of the two,it was a discovery of a major importance and one which I now had to live with. With a determined effort to keep the descending murkiness at bay,I delved into the innermost recesses of my mental store and secreted this new found knowledge as deep as possible, burying it amongst all my other concealed deposits. Unfortunately,and in the belief that my illness was life threatening, I became enmeshed in a curtain of physcological drama, so much so, that for the first time in my life, Jimmy Brown, the great advocate of optimism,came face to face with the champion of defeatism; self pity.

C H A P T E R   S E V E N

Peeling the potatoes,enough to fill three large buckets,was a hated chore,similar to the cleaning of all the boots and shoes. Both these jobs took up valuable playing-out time and both were apportioned to the prime period of Saturday af -ternoon,especially if it was given as a punishment for mis-behaviour. Looking back to that day in early summer, when serving out a penance for something I had or hadn't done, I was unaware that the next few hours were about to turn my world upside down. Sat on an upturned vegetable box, a sack of potatoes on one side and three buckets of water on the other, I huddled under the shadow of the outside fire-escape and the outside wall, viewing the antics of my pals playing 'King of the Castle' on top of the now obsolete air-raid shelter. Careful not to let the water and peelings run down the apron onto my legs, I methodically checked each and every potato before throwing it into the bucket. From past experience I knew only too well that leaving any eyes in the finished product would create another confrontation and poss -ibly another early bedtime. It was at this exact moment, a daydreaming transitory type of moment when meditation and wishing abstracts produced the right blend of indifference, that a distant voice penetrated my deliberations. "A visitor for Jimmy Brown. A visitor for Jimmy Brown." The bearer of this bulletin, an older girl belonging to the Lodge Home, de -livered her Saturday afternoon message both to anyone who could relay her communique and also to the housemother who was on duty. How many times over the years had I listened to the same familiar despatch on a Saturday afternoon, and how many times had I ignored the episode on the very certain assumption that visitors were always for someone else. Maybe,this really was my lucky day, and perhaps a wish had finally come true for 'Jimmy Wish Wish'. If indeed there was a visitor for me,how was I going to react to this new chapter of events? My new line of thinking had no sooner originated when the order came from Miss Chedley to drop everything I was doing and "go and wash,and change into Sunday best", a command which helped in stabilizing my thoughts. An inspection by the home mother which assured the onlooker that I'd washed behind my ears, combed my hair, and generally presented a good image as an ambassador of 'N' Home,was the climax to the unfolding destiny. My faltering footsteps en-route to the Lodge were an indication of my apprehensiveness and I became aware of other children staring at me as I made my way to the front gates of the colony. Blushing from extreme shyness as I became exposed to the change in fortune, I reflected on the visiting ritual of which I myself, had often been a part, when,along with groups of other children,we would peer from behind the rhododendron bushes in an effort to catch a glimpse of a make believe relative. On one occasion, when searching for a kind face or even a kind response, I remember being rewarded with a bag of sweets,which to my dismay,instantly disappeared under an avalanche of tiny sweaty palms.

Following the bend of Church Avenue to the juncture of the church and the Boss's house, I peered anxiously towards the wooden bench situated in front of the Lodge. If there were any visitors and it was a nice day such as today,then that is where they would be sat. I could make out the figure of my sister Vera because of her long golden hair and,the dress which signified a Styal Homes inmate,but as yet,the visitors accompanying her were complete strangers. "Guess who's come to see us?" said Vera, with a smile of excitement written on her face. "It's our Father, and Sylvia. They've just gone in to sign the visitors book." So infectious was Vera's elation that she took hold of my hand and put her other arm around my shoulder,triggering an intimacy of brotherly and sisterly affection which neither of us had previously shared. Conscious that a 'girl' was holding my hand,and that other boys might be watching from the hideouts in the church gardens, I pulled away from my sister hoping that the encounter had gone unnoticed otherwise,I would become subjected to the taunts of 'cissy' for weeks to come. "Look Jimmy, our names are on the slate board" said Vera,pointing to the girl standing by the hedgerow,a slate in one hand and a long piece of white chalk in the other. Staring at the familiar notice board,an item which until now had been of no importance, I observed the bold inscription which stated: A VISITOR FOR; and then underneath,a list of names proclaiming the good providence of the fortunate few. There it was,underlined,and about three rows from the top; 'VERA BROWN - JIMMY BROWN'. Interrupting my gaze,Vera gave me a nudge,and with the same smile on her face,pointed to the couple emerging from the doorway of the Lodge. "There's your Dad." My first reaction on seeing the tall bespectacled elderly man dressed smartly in a grey suit,was to distance myself from what looked like being an awkward confrontation,and as if sensing my shyness, Vera again nudged me and pointed to the well dressed lady alongside him saying, "and that's your big sister Sylvia." Reflecting on that day,as I have done over the years, it was perhaps too big an occasion for my young mind to cope with. If there was a standard routine which applied to father and son meeting for the first time,then I was completely lost. However, having resorted to instinct in preference to a set agenda, I edged closer to my new found family to offer a polite response to the accolades now descending around my upright shoulders. It was obvious that my father was frail, and as Vera ordered him to sit on the bench,I became aware of his laboured breathing,the result I assumed, of his war disability and the long walk from the Styal bus terminus. During this conflict of emotions,I had recieved a hug and a kiss from Sylvia and for one brief moment,her smile had reassured me that not only was she aware of my circumstances but like myself shared in a togetherness of sensitivity and compassion. My father on the other hand,was a sick man,even to my immature observations,and although his overall smart appearance belied his condition,the ageing process showed in his every rhythm. The trilby which remained perched on his head for most of the afternoon was, I assumed,either a cover for his greying baldness or a simple means to keep the chill off his head. Somehow, his whole image seemed to portray a likeness to one of the characters in a silent film that had recently been shown, a gentle,intellectual gentleman,who for one reason or another,had reached that critical stage of one's life,either through bad health or bad luck. "Your Dads been to the Ship Inn for a drink and a sandwich" said Sylvia "and guess who he was talking to, - Mr Mottershead." That would explain the unfamiliar smell on his breath when he attempted to kiss my cheek, recalling that first embrace. Unpleasant as it was, the scratching of my face from his wiry bristles coupled with the ingrained tobacco odours on his clothing, became secondary to the importance of our first family get together.

The 'Homes' children of Styal were nearly all familiar with the visit and visitor routine, in that a visit by a relative usually became synonymous with gifts and other treats, and with this thought uppermost in my mind,my eyes searched for the tell-tale signs of carrier bags or wrapping paper. As if reading my thoughts,my father put his arm across my shoulder and asked me to lift the brown paper bag onto his knee. "It isn't much,but it's all I could afford to bring" he said, in his quiet manner. "Go on, open it." Blushing from all the attention from my onlookers,I slowly undid the string to reveal its surprise contents. I had never seen a Gyrocopter before now, in fact I had never heard of an aeroplane which resembled the picture featured on the side of the wrapping. It certainly was an unusual present, and my excitement on discovering that the key winding mechanism operated two over-head propellers,erupted into a show of complete gratitude. Overcome with emotional appreciation and holding back the instinctive threat of tears, I nodded a very meaningful thank

-you. I really couldn't thank him enough for a present that not only represented the best possession that I had ever had but one which must have cost a lot of money. Remembering his remark about being able to afford it, provoked another line of thought and for one brief moment,a guilt feeling invaded my selfish euphoria. Having been given sufficient time in which to savour my new acquisition, another parcel was handed to me by Sylvia. Placing it on the seat,she said;"I hope you like it Jimmy, that's from me." My eyes bulged at the sight of the big parcel,causing further excitement to course through my veins in anticipation of yet another treasure trove. Once inside, the top layer of the box revealed a cake covered with a layer of icing and an inscription which spelled out my name. "That's for your tea when you get back, now look underneath the cake." Exposing the bottom half of the parcel, I lifted out a bundle of bound books and observed that it represented a cross section of my favourite comic material. At that moment,it never occurred to me to ask her how she knew of my preferences, probably because I was too overwhelmed with the knowledge that I now had enough books to last me for some weeks to come. On top of that, I also knew that I had acquired enough potential with which to make swaps for all sorts of things from the other boys. In spite of his tired appearance,my father suggested a walk down to Styal village,assuring us that the fresh country air would do him a power of good. Having deposited the parcels at the Lodge for safe keeping, Sylvia insisted that we should have a photograph taken with her new box camera. Finalising the group photo session with a picture of myself and Vera,stood at the entrance gates to the colony, the last hour of the afternoon visit drew to its close all too quickly, and the final curtain on the proceedings was all that remained between me,and the most memorable day in my life. That ever so slow return walk from Robinson's sweet shop became riveted in my mind as I clung to the memory of my father linking his arms with Vera and Sylvia and also, at my additional fortune manifested by the bulging pocket of sweets and the bottle of dandelion and burdock. "Its time to go,Jimmy." As I acknowledged this remark by Sylvia,I glanced back to observe Vera engrossed in a final hug with my father. Compelled by the system to live like strangers,even though we only lived a short distance from each other, Vera and I never ever got close enough to each other to display any show of feelings or emotions and now, seeing the tears running down her rosy cheeks and genuine sorrow written in her face, I too became infected with the same heartbreak. By the time Sylvia had come to my rescue with her immaculate white handkerchief, I noticed that she too was finding difficulty in holding back her sentiments. Clutching hold of Sylvia in an attempt to prevent the inevitable,it became more obvious that unless someone showed the strength of courage to rise above the occasion,the only other option was more heartbreak. My Father's "dry your eyes now,and be a good boy"was sufficient to quell the tide of emotion,and realising that this was just the right moment to grasp her own lifeline, Sylvia proclaimed also that if they didn't leave at that moment,they would miss the return bus to Manchester. Bewildered by all that had transpired, my fragile emotions underwent a further trauma when, at teatime that same evening,the housemother ordered my cake to be sliced into enough pieces for all the children of the Home to share. In a state of anger,mainly from having lost my cake and being forced to share-out my comic books, I went to bed reflecting on all the good and bad aspects of my day, especially,on the memories of my father,and sister Sylvia. Fortunately,I had taken the wise precaution of hiding my new Gyrocopter in my secret hiding place, thus ensuring that my Dad's gift would remain my best and only possession.

In complete contrast to the routines of the previous five or six years, the summer of 1946,according to the rife gossip, was going to see the resumption of the annual seaside holiday. Rumours and childish excitement had been building for some months,causing not only a rise in the level of morale but an increased output from the overworked storytellers. Without too much effort,I can bring to mind one of the early morning school parades of that year when, in an attempt to quell the heresay concerning the holidays,the Boss commanded everybody in the colony to attend an important announcement. What transpired next,took everybody by surprise as the sober 'Colonel Blimp' figure of Superintendent,flanked on either side by the Matron and his wife, stepped onto a raised platform holding aloft a sheaf of papers. "This is NOT,A PRISON. Styal Homes,is NOT,A PRISON." Except for the intermittent cawing of the woodland crows, there was an awesome silence that defied any adult or child to breach. I had never seen the Boss in such a stern mood before now and it was obvious that he was treating the matter in hand as a very serious issue. Separating the papers and holding aloft a selection for everyone to see, he continued: "I am not going to mention the persons by name,but some of you have been writing to outside relatives describing your life here as being like that of a prisoner in a prison. This will not be tolerated. The next person found spreading these malicious lies will be punished. Now then, about the seaside holidays this year." The sudden change in mood and direction came as a great relief to the assembly,whilst at the same time,giving me a moment in which to reflect on the 'prison' statement. Who, I questioned,would have the audacity let alone the courage to tell anyone on the outside about conditions in the Homes. It must be someone who hasn't been here for very long otherwise they would have known that all letters posted within the institution were subject to being opened before going through the gates. In his continuation of the holiday bulletin, the Boss confirmed that the holiday destination for this year would be the North Wales resort of Colwyn and Abergele,where, the girls would spend two weeks and the boys, a separate two weeks. From that moment on, talk of the holiday chalet accommodation took preference to any other topic and all that remained before the big day,was an informal gathering at the recreational hall for notification of travel proceedures. For some reason,probably a reminder of past disappointments, a niggling doubt began to invade my confidence suggesting that maybe,I wouldn't be eligible for a holiday. Brushing aside my natural desire to show anxiety for something that had not yet happened, I assured myself that because of my di-sease, allowances would probably be made for me. Convinced by this logic, I watched patiently as all the children responded to the roll call and individually,attended the briefing concerning departure proceedures. Eventually,there remained a fragmented group of young girls and boys who, for one reason or another,found themselves isolated in the big hall,each of them awaiting their fate. Believing these circumstances to be an ominous indication of what was to come next,each of us took our turn in answering the summons to an area near to the stage where,our respective fate was made known. When my turn came for the brief face to face,it was reminiscent of past disappointments where sympathetic leanings became the forerunner of impending bad news. "I don't have to tell you,Jimmy Brown,you are old enough to know that until you put an end to your bad habit,you wont be going any-where. Why dont you try." This last sentence,uttered more as a question,put an end to any further rhetoric as I blindly made a hurried retreat out of the building. There was only one answer to this colossal bombshell and that, was the safety and solitude of my den near the river. "How could it happen to me,again? Why am I always being punished?" From the seclusion in the undergrowth, my heart now burdened with a renewed hatred of the system,I reflected on a future which could and would,only find solace in the one remaining option - my escape from Styal 'prison'.

Whether from sympathy,or as a result of the sudden drop in

population,the routine for those who were excluded from the exodus became relaxed,almost to the point of being excused from all work timetables. Pardoned from this drudgery,if on -ly temporarily,did compensate for the loss of a holiday,and even the so-called essential jobs such as filling palliases with straw became a lighthearted pastime. The Homes work-yard,normally a thriving hub of industry, became strangely deserted in the wake of the summer recess,and now,accentuated by the absence of its artisans,its appeal,from an inquisitive point of view,grew more fascinating. To my mind, the cobbled work area where the horses were led into the stables represented a very friendly part of the colony mainly, as a result of the personalities of three of its employees. Out of this trio,one in particular appealed to my limited sense of humour,and in spite of his scruffy dirty appearance from working in polluted atmospheres, he had a vibration about him that spelled warmth and understanding. Over a period of time,including the months ahead, Thomas Lyle the overalled assistant of Mr Mottershead,would prove that with his unique sense of perception he could not only communicate with young children but also share in their private sufferings. In con -trast to the intellectual and seemingly knowledgable Amos Lyle, another man who shared the toasting fork routine round the brazier was the carter,Tommy Shatwell. His,was the job of transporting all the food and other provisions to all the houses by way of his horse and cart. Known for his fondness for shire horses in particular,Mr Shatwell was less inclined to conversation than his associates,preferring instead to

transmit short sharp commands to his beasts of burden. Due to a kick on his leg by a previous horse, he walked with a limp,an impediment which reduced his stature and characterised his individuality. In spite of his regular attempts to keep children from interfering with the mechanics and danger of horse and cart paraphinalia, he would also on numerous occasions, allow the little ones to hitch a ride on the back of the cart,a gesture that sowed many a seed of gratefulness.
"I want you to go to the village today to get my errands." This request by Miss Chedley appeared to signify that I was now mature and old enough to attempt my first shopping venture to the village of Styal,although more than likely, it was because I was the only boy available. Carrying the old wicker basket containing a list of items and an envelope con -taining some money,I slowly made my way along Styal Road, carefully keeping a safe distance from the entrance gates to Bailey's Farm. There was a sheepdog at the farm which was renowned for its barking at strangers and being frightened of dogs,a fact borne out when I hid behind my sister Vera on the occasion of my father's visit, I was more than ready for a rapid retreat. More than likely, the dog was being over affectionate,but because of my upbringing,any animal apart from a cat,was an alien species that threatened danger. The first item on the list was a bag of pears from Hope's Farm,a bonus for me,since Miss Hope who worked at the Homes recognized me and gave me some bruised pears for my trouble. Next on the list was Mr Mottram's shoe shop where a parcel of repaired shoes would be ready for collection. Posting the two

letters at Earlam's post office opposite the Ship Inn was my last but one assignment before heading for the sprawling garden centre owned by Mr Leah. Here,according to Miss Chedley,was the only place of any note at which flowers should be bought, especially 'sweet williams' and 'carnations',her favourite blooms. Thinking back to something Amos Lyle had once mentioned about the contents of peoples privvies in the village dwellings being emptied on to the local garden allot -ments became uppermost in my mind as I surveyed the flowers and breathed the stench of manure. Walking back in the direction of Hollin Lane,I paused at the roadside facing the empty cricket field and stood in my favourite spot beneath the old gnarled tree. "Surely, they wouldn't put that kind of fertilizer on the vegetable patches,would they?" Dismiss -ing this possibility as complete nonsense I returned to the matters in hand and proceeded in my retreat to the colony, observing the village from my hedgerow surveillance. "I wish I could ride a bicycle. I wish we could have bicycles in the Homes, then I could learn to ride." Here I was again,indulging in my number one pastime. "It just doesn't seem fair. Everybody has a bike in the village, even the boys and girls Maybe when I become grown up and leave Styal,somebody will give me a go on theirs. I wouldn't even mind if it was all rusty or dirty or, even if it was a ladies bike, so long as I could have a go." My train of thought had been triggered by the sight of P.C.Waite,the village policeman,who had just mounted his bike in front of his house on Altrincham Road. My face coloured up as he rode past, not that I had anything to hide or be conscience stricken about, it was my normal re -action to go red in the face and assume a guilt feeling if I was confronted by an official,especially a uniformed one. For a few moments,my mind went back to the 'visit' as I rem-embered Vera's comments about PC.Waite when she and her pals had been apprehended for raiding a fruit orchard. I smiled as I recalled her'dramatic'account of the incident showing how her pinafore dress had been tucked into her knickers in an effort to conceal the pile of apples. She didn't say if she had received a punishment, but knowing the reputation of PC Waite,she would more than likely have been cautioned and told not to do it again. "When I run away, he'll be the one who'll fetch me back. He's always bringing runaways back to the Homes." With a transfer of thought in the wake of the policeman's disappearance, I mused on the recent spate of ab -sconding by the boys and girls of the Homes, the result, I had been informed, of the new disciplinary rules which had been issued by the Manchester Town Hall. Strong rumours had flowed freely amongst the colony's residents for some time about home mothers who had rejected orders to abandon their practice of hitting children and had retaliated by walking out of the establishment. To my mind and from my own exper-ience,this particular story lacked substance and was dismiss -ed from my mind as being just another fib.

The final day of the summer holidays, a Saturday morning in late August was,I remember,one of those days which seemed to climax the voluptuous nature on the one hand and the renewed optimism -the effects of my long hiliday- on the other.

Armed with a vigour for the day's promising adventures ahead I completed my jobs of work in double quick time,whilst making certain that there would be no reason for the assistant housemother to call me back. There was just one final errand but since it was at the hospital,I could use the same route to continue to my chosen destination, be it a raid on the orchards at Stanneylands, chasing the horses up and down the fields, or swimming in the Bollin. The latter,because of a threatening humidity, became an easy choice,and with the argument now settled,I made my way along the hospital avenue, under a cloud of daydreams. Having acquired an old rubber ball from under the hedgerow,I continued my journey in tune to the most irregular of bounces from an object that had out lived its usefulness a long time ago. As if to prove that I had judged wrongly,the ball shot into the air and disappeared over the hedge where,from my view through the branches,it had landed on some grass. Without thinking too much of the consequences,I climbed onto the rickety fence and jumped over the prickly hawthorns to make what I thought was a perfect landing. Too late! Even without knowledge or experience,I realized that this was no ordinary grass. The col -our, a bright synthetic green,should have told me, as well, as the unusual smoothness of the lawn like surface. As soon as my sandals disappeared beneath the spongy smelly trifle I could only think of one word; 'bog'. Unhurried,due to the fact that as yet the seriousness of the situation hadn't registered,I struggled to reach hold of a branch alongside the banking, an effort that only served to increase the sinking momentum. The fact that I couldn't reach the embankment and the effects of the suction having swallowed my legs almost to my waist,caused such a fright at the realization of my predicament that a blind panic began to set in. Knowing that my location was off the beaten track and likely to be deserted, especially on a Saturday afternoon, I began to shout aloud the word "help",in a voice that was very near to tears. Aware that my situation was now critical,and my fate,nearing a crisis that had come all too soon in my life,I shouted for all I was worth,hoping beyond hope that someone somewhere in the colony would respond. "What's up,Jimmy? What's all the noise about." This seemingly casual interruption by Brian Wilson,an acqaintance from one of the other boy's homes, had the immediate effect of diffusing the trauma,and the relief as he handed me a branch to grasp a lifeline,was one of deep gratitude. The arrival back at the Home had all the makings of yet another trauma as I surveyed my shoeless,mucky state. Smelling like Park's farmyard,I hesitantly knocked on the front door,ready with an explanation that I was convinced would earn me a sympathetic hearing. The truth,no matter how it was presented,collapsed in pieces as the assistant housemother reacted with a venomous onslaught of blows to my head. "Stop those lies at once,and go and bath yourself. When you are in a fit state to leave the house you can go to the shoe shop and tell him I sent you. See if he believes you. Do you hear me?" "Yis M'm, yis M'm, I replied,as I made a hurried exit from the corridor. Mr Gillison,the senior shoemaker of the Styal colony's thriving industry,was a man of few words.

To my complete surprise,the explanation I gave for losing my sandals was not only accepted without punishment but even re -warded with the offer of a replacement pair from the stock-pile of repaired footwear. Sitting on the bench to remove the tight fitting boots I had borrowed,I breathed a sigh of relief as I kicked off the heavy burdens. Crack! The foll-owing second,I was lying on the floor nursing a bruised face and an equally bruised pride. "That'll teach you to take off your shoes without undoing the laces first." In fear of any further discipline I quickly reseated my anatomy and obeyed every instruction in silent anger. With a brooding resent-ment at having experienced his reputation at first hand, I retreated from the building with my mind firmly made up. The strange ringing noise in my ear and the bruising on my head became minor details as I reflected on the physical assault which I now viewed as being the very last straw. It was now or never,I decided,to run away for ever from this rotten old prison and never come back. "I know," thinking out aloud, "I'll go to the stables after dinner and sit in the hay and decide on my plan of action for the escape." Lying comfort-ably on the straw strewn floor of the barn,the afternoon re-fuge became a safe haven of pleasant fragrances, where the warmth of the afternoon sun mingled with the peace and tran-quility of a better world. "Was it to be Wilmslow,or was it to be Styal,once I was outside the gates?" This question, and the daunting challenge which would confront me once I be came a free agent in an alien environment,was becoming more problematic than my immediate circumstances. Seeking sanctuary from the turmoil that was my mind,I closed my eyes and attached myself to one of my mythical floating clouds of cot-ton-wool daydreams. Over the years,these heavenly flagships had rescued me from many a stressful situation and now,as a matter of routine,my subconscious enabled me to step on or off this celestial stairway. The strange voices and the in-termittent fits of giggling became noisy intruders to the closing chapter of the afternoon as I woke to the commotion below me. Refreshed from my slumber,I cautiously crept to the loft entrance and peered down at a group of four or five older girls. My first reaction was to question the girls in-telligence and stupidity for standing so close to the cart-horse,let alone being inside the stables. I had always been under the impression that girls were frightened to death of such big horses,and that men and boys were the natural mast-ers of these beasts. What happened next,and what caused me to blink in disbelief,was something so strange,so primitive, so crudely exciting,that each moment of discovery contribut-ed to a surge of sexual arousement. Stimulated by the unus-ual scene below, I watched intently as the leading girl held out a long stem of straw to the undercarriage of the horses' rear end. Unfortunately, my aerial viewpoint prevented any clear vision of how the horse was reacting to the girl's out-stretched advances,but since it was obvious that the horses' intimate parts were the object of all the attention,it could be assumed that something would happen sooner or later. The excitement in the voices of the girls suggested that they had achieved their objective and as if to prove a point,they rotated their positions to allow each one to take turns with the offending piece of straw. A few moments later,the girls and the giggling disappeared from the stables and I was able to observe the enormous hosepipe like stem which had claimed the girls attention. Lying in bed that same night,I reflected on what should have been my final hours following yet again another decision to escape the institutional regime. If it hadn't been for the distraction at the stables I might now have been at the critical planning stages. Admitting my weakness,especially where the opposite sex was concerned, I abandoned my escape ritual in favour of the exciting memory of that afternoon.

A group of boys from Nut Cottage.

C H A P T E R   E I G H T

As always,September signalled the three major events which were synonymous with that time of year. The first,being my birthday, the second,conker collecting,and the third,Harvest festival,an event whch caused me to reflect on Miss Chedley. Year in and year out,along with two other home-mothers,Miss Chedley took on the responsibility of decorating the church with the produce from the school gardens. More often than not,the flowers and the fruit came from the village, and it was rumoured that Miss Chedley spent her own money on these supplements. It was also common knowledge amongst the adult staff that the skills and artistry of flower arranging for each Sunday service not only brightened up the interior on a grey day,but also advertised the individual talents of that particular person. As I grew older,so too did the elderly home-mother, and my feelings towards this ageing disciplin-arian mellowed with each passing year. Miss Chedley appeared to be as timeless as the village of Styal and yet,there were obvious signs that with all the rumoured changes about to take effect within the colony,her days were becoming number-ed. In spite of the fact that she had been the only mother I had ever known,and that she had been responsible for a ma-jor part of my unhappiness, I couldn't help but look back on this period with a sympathy and compassion that belied my own frustrations. It was now,that time of the year again, a time when the receeding summer refused to quicken its foot-steps and autumn,playing a waiting game,stood idly by before determing its own grand entrance. Schooling,during the aut-umn term,meant that for the senior boys,potato picking harvest time had arrived,and since I was now a senior grade boy, I was eligible to join the ranks of the mature work force as a 'potato picker'. Viewed as a soft option by the majority, this alternative to school-room drudgery proved to be little more than yet another back breaking chore. There was however one striking difference between this job of work and all the other jobs of work; a wage. As a result of my promotion and good fortune,I was now in the position to earn one penny for every hour of potato picking and this,added to my Saturday pocket money of another penny,increased my weekly income to the astonishing figure of tenpence a week. My morale boosted with this new found wealth,albeit short lived,acquired a new dimension especially at weekends when Saturday afternoon vis -its to Wilmslow were permitted. Woolworths, the target of every Home's child who wandered down Grove Street,was a won-derland of well stocked counters,where dreams could become reality for those with money in their pockets. For the maj-ority who had little or no money,Woolworths proved time and time again as it had done over many years,to be the fatal a-ttraction that had caused the downfall of many an inmate of Styal Homes, My introduction to this episode came about one Saturday afternoon after returning from a shopping adventure that had included some packets of foreign stamps from Sant's Newsagents in Church street,and some varied items from Wool-worths. "Empty your pockets." This order from the Boss was addressed to a group of boys and girls including myself, who were stood in a line-up outside the main lodge house. It be came obvious from the tone of his voice that this parade was nothing more than an exercise to find out if the items found in the person's possession were legitimate or not. With his humour showing in his smile as he inspected the many worthless articles, I hesitated at producing my purchases in case he didn't believe me and confiscated all that I had bought. Fortunately on this occasion, he accepted my explanations but it was obvious from the bag he was carrying that some of the others hadn't passed the test and their so-called purchases would be returned to the shop in question.

To any former child of the Styal colony, one memory will last them to the end of their life. Pausing for a moment to reflect on this interruption to my sequence of recollections, I focussed my attention on the seemingly endless hours of walking to school and back, along the Styal road. There are two thousand four hundred walking paces between the parade area of the Homes and the school at the village. With firm conviction, I know this to be true, since I have counted on numerous occasions my marching footsteps to the school and back. Done initially as an exercise to occupy my mind along the endless footpath, I concluded this answer after very many attempts at trying to find the right one, thus, not only did I improve my arithmetic skills but also discovered something that in all probability, no one else had even thought of.
On the one hand, finding out the answer had provided me with a sense of achievement and a certain amount of pride in that, I could tell the world that a Styal school pupil walking to school and back twice a day for a week, would most probably take a total of forty eight thousand footsteps. Looking at

the other side of the coin and the new found knowledge instigated by my mental wanderings,I also became aware of wasted time on a piece of useless information that was really of no use to anyone.

The annual church choir outing in early September will for ever be remembered if only for its date, a time in my life when the world was turned upside down and my whole future,placed in jeopardy. From the weather's point of view,it was a day to be cherished with warm sunshine stealing a few more precious hours from its seasonal expiry date. In terms of distance,Alderley Edge lay only a few short miles from the village of Wilmslow and in my own view,didn't qualify as a proper description for an outing. However, from my own experience,outings were a rare occurrance and as the trek got under way from outside the Rex cinema,I began my excursion into the unknown with a great excitement. Weary and fatigued after the long climb up the steep hill,the Edge,with its superb views across the plains,offered an interval of freedom from the back packs and a refuge for all the tired and weary. The next item on the agenda after the sandwiches and bottles of 'pop' had been demolished,was a visit to the near by copper mine. In Styal,as probably in Wilmslow,tales of Alderly Edge copper mines were legendary and as I followed the others into the dark recesses I searched by candlelight for the tell-tale signs of roman endeavours. The history,as explained by Mr Taylor,is long forgotten,but somewhere in my old den in Styal Woods,are pieces of rock which,because of their green mould appearance,authenticates them as being the genuine copper mineral. Before descending into Alderley, a surprise stop at the Wizard Tea Rooms for tea and cakes was the reward for being well behaved and since there was every likelihood of having to walk the whole of the distance back to the Homes, the meal became an incentive to raise morale.

Word of the Boss's crow shooting which had taken place during my Saturday outing, had spread through the grapevine until it was common knowledge. Supposedly, he had shot down about a hundred birds but the reality was more like twenty or so. To the more knowledgeable like myself, half of the birds would be dead before they hit the ground and the other dozen would end up being maimed and wounded and become easy prey for the stick wielding crow hunters. It was now Tuesday pm; the potato picking had been completed and there was "just about time" according to Wooksie, "to catch some lame crows before teatime." "Jimmy Brown!" From beneath the undergrowth in the woods I silently cursed at the intrusion and hoped that whoever wanted me would keep clear of my hiding place. "I know you're hiding. Miss Chedley says you've got to go at once. It's urgent." Before he could shout another "Jimmy Brown" I rose up from my hideout and said I would go at once. "She's probably found out that I've finished early for the day and wants me to do some extra work." This line of thinking continued as I made my way to the Home and just as the house came into view another barrage of choruses met my arrival. "Jimmy Brown, Jimmy Brown, you're wanted by Miss Chedley." By the time I arrived at the doorway I was convinced that I had done something wrong, and my face had begun to change to its guilty colour of beetroot in anticipation. "Just look at the state of you. Go and wash yourself clean and then come and see me in my parlour." By the time I had finished the cleansing process I had convinced myself that I must have a visitor. Why else would I be told to look clean so early before teatime? Another thought occurred to me."It might be something to do with the scholarship. Maybe they've found me somewhere to live." A gentle tapping on the house mother's door signified that I was ready and presentable and as I inspected my scrubbed hands and knees I became more and more convinced that something out of the ordinary was imminent. Passing the brief inspection,Miss Chedley pointed to a large easy chair next to the open fireplace and ordered me to sit comfortably. Taking in as much detail of her parlour as was possible,I fixed my gaze on the large glass vase that contained the perfumed 'sweet william's'. "This must be how a real home would look like", I thought, as I experienced a strange unsettling degree of cosiness from the soft but firm cushions of the armchair. "This,must be how a home in heaven would look, all bright and cheerful,with flowers and decorative wallpaper and curtains,with sunbeams filtering warming rays of spiritual hospitality." Cutting short my daydreams Miss Chedley gave a cough as she seated herself in what appeared to be her favourite fireside chair. "I'm afraid I've got some bad news for you." A long pause followed. "Your father's dead." For a brief moment,in fact,for what seemed an everlastng moment,the news failed to register a response. "How am I supposed to react? How do I respond to this bombshell?" In the mental confusion that surfaced and resurface-ed,a picture of my father sat on the bench outside the Home Lodge building became clearer in my mind. His trilby tilted to one side from my efforts to playfully dislodge his attire, his legs crossed in a relaxed pose as he leaned backwards to take a puff from his rolled-up cigarette,became memories of such prominence that I fought hard to cling on to them. As the news bulletin began to take effect,a wave of emotion began to sweep over me causing a solitary tear to run slowly down my face. "Did you understand what I've just said?" I nodded my head at Miss Chedley and said; "yes M'm." Sensing that I needed some kind of comfort and relief from what was proving to be a very delicate interlude, Miss Chedley stood up and beckoned me to go to her. No sooner had I nestled my head against her blue uniform and yielded to the firmness of her arm pressing me into her bosom,when the dam burst,causing a deluge of tears and an accompaniment of loud cries. The tears continued to flow as if there was no stopping them and I sensed Miss Chedley's frustration at what appeared to be a situation that was getting out of hand. "That's enough of that, you never knew your father, so why all the tears? Pull yourself together and dry your eyes." Taking the handkerchief from her, I attempted to mop the tears between each interval of heavy sobbing whilst at the same time inwardly questioning her decision to bring down the final curtain on my bereavement. Very many times and over a period of many months since the paternal loss of my father,I have reflected on my behaviour in Miss Chedley's living room. Telling me that I hadn't known my father had seemed cruel and unsympathetic and yet,her statement had contained a certain element of truth. Just why,I had cried continually had been totally perplexing to me as it had to Miss Chedley and the very same question had persisted throughout the remaining years of my confinement. Almost three years were to pass before the an--swer came to me. In fact, the day it occurred, just over a month before my release,was one of those clear headed days when every thought and question going through my mind found a simple solution almost instantanously. Staring me in the face,was an image of Miss Chedley,her arms around my shoulders and a strange but nice feeling of something I had never experienced; love and affection. That, I concluded,was the reason I had broken down,and the dam of tears that had gushed out in such force was the reaction to a show of seemingly genuine compassion. Just like an imaginary house of picture cards collapsing,other images became exposed until finally, like a blueprint,the answer mirrored the reality of it all. Firstly,there was the stark contrast between Miss Chedley's living room and the cold bareness of the children's facilities. The homelike appearance from the brightly furnished lounge,supplemented by the sweet smelling blooms,differed so much from the sterile surroundings of the remainder of the house that the encounter became like a soothing anesthetic, subduing everything and everybody. My conclusion, was that whilst temporary under the influence of the tranquil climate, Miss Chedley's show of tenderness caught me unaware and her embrace was the key which unlocked my imprisoned emotions.

I had now reached a milestone in my life,not that I was know -ledgeable about such matters,but it was becoming obvious to me that some inner force,probably to do with my age and maturity,was projecting me,like the approaching winter, towards some form of conclusion. In my search for answers to life's purpose especially my own circumstances,the resentment and anger grew so intense that I began to feel very bitter about everything the institution stood for. For the first time in my life I felt the pangs of rebellion against the punishment, the system,the commands,the school headmaster,and everything else. The urge to run away was now stronger than it had ever been but again,caution intervened and I decided that in view of winter being just around the corner,it would have to be postponed temporarily. Besides, according to rumour, there was going to be a Guy Fawkes night of entertainment,and what with the prospect of fun and fireworks around a bonfire and an opportunity to steal a kiss and hold hands with a girl in the darkness, the springtime of next year was a far better option.

Styal, like every other town and village in the country,had its worst winter for decades and according to the wisdom of Thomas Lyle,1947 would probably set new records for the area. I can just picture him now, sitting on his upturned wooden box next to the brazier,a toasting fork in one hand and his billy-can in the other. "By 'eck, its a cold 'un this year." That remark made in the workmen's den,seemed to sum up the whole picture of what was to be one of the longest winters on record. From the children's point of view there were two ways of looking at it. On the one hand,there was the white winter wonderland of exciting adventures when skating, snowballing,building snowmen and tobogganing,produced hours of untold pleasure. For the older juveniles,a more enjoyable menu became available by way of the Black Lake at Lindow Com -mon where the water had been transformed into a skaters par -adise. Another temptation and one shared by the Wilmslow communities in general,was the popular Carrs Wood hillside which,when frosted over by winter conditions,produced a hard natural surface slide from top to bottom. The other side of the coin was more serious in view of the arctic conditions and keeping warm became the number one priority. The two warmest places in the home were the kitchen and dining room where,in the latter,an open fire thawed out cold limbs and revived flagging spirits. Climbing out of bed in the early dawn and standing barefoot on the cold flooring,an everyday normal routine, was suddenly transformed into a race against time to dress into some warm clothing. With no end in sight and the harsh winter conditions continuing,the shivering and teeth chattering became a morning chorus in the halflight of the chilled dormitory. Making the trek to the ablutions a-cross the frozen snow became another ordeal but knowing that all the other children from the other homes were sharing in the same hardship and experiencing the same frozen toilets, somehow compensated matters. In any case, if like me, with thoughts of the breakfast of hot porridge topped with a tea-spoon of sugar spurring me on,the ordeal would evaporate in anticipation of that first warming spoonful of sweet gruel.

"I wish we could have long trousers in the winter." This, one of my reccuring wishes over the past few years,signified my yearning for some form of warmer clothing throughout the coldest months of the year. Observing the unusually high proportion of children who were displaying the tell-tale signs of chapped hands and chapped legs,I became more and more convinced that a long pair of trousers would compensate the life threatening bleak winter. Peeling potatoes, a routine chore hated by every boy in the home had, owing to the acute weather,become more burdensome with every touch of the cold implements. Whilst reflecting on my own spate of chapping, the results of my own encounters associated with domesticity, my thoughts went back to a recent incident concerning my pal Wooksie. Turning back the clock to that day at school when Wooksie,probably due to his sometimes obstinate nature, had been summonsed to stand outside Smiggy's office,I became sickened with absolute fear as I listened to his screams echoing down the corridor. Unlike me,Wooksie could absorb a good hiding and not flicker an eyelid but on this occasion it became very obvious that Smiggy's stick had finally broken his resilience. His return to the classroom had the effect of silencing the rest of the pupils and as always,following the return of a punished individual,fear was the key to the ensuing obedience. Out of the corner of my eye I could see the tearstained face of my sobbing pal and as he raised his arm to wipe his nose on his sleeve,I saw the reason behind his submission;a chapped hand that was both swollen and bleeding At that point,I hated Smiggy more than anything else in the whole world. It had been rumoured only recently that he was now using the sticks of wood which had been the stabilizers in the window blinds used during the war time black-outs. Prompted by what I had just witnessed in relation to Wooksie I reminded myself that "this year,I am definitely going to run away,only this time,I really mean it."

Monday nights in the wintertime were set aside for what was commonly known as 'darning night' and after the teatime dut-ies had been completed and the younger children sent up the stairs to bed,the dining room come play room was transformed into a work room. According to heresay, this Monday night ritual of needlework was a tradition which stretched back to the begining of the colony and one which ensured that every Home's child going out into the world would be capable of darning their own socks. Supervising the proceedings,the ho-me mother would empty a pile of washed socks onto the comm-unal tables followed by large balls of grey wool and a quan-tity of shaped wooden mushrooms. For the next two hours the silent concentration became stifling as the homemother made her way around the tables inspecting the work. If the comp-leted job of work passed her scrutiny then a pat on the head and a compliment would be the reward,otherwise,it was rejec-ted and ordered to be cut out and started all over again.
The new year brought a host of changes amongst the staffing of the colony, and rumours throughout the juvenile population centered on the resignations of the so-called 'older' Home Mothers. In this category was the unfortunate Miss Chedley who's demise passed as if she had never existed,and sad as I

had been to see her go,there was something refreshing about the new younger element of authority. Taking over from the old hierarchy were two new housemothers of quite opposite di -mensions. One,a very young lady of slim proportions who's attractive features hid behind her bespectacled stern looks, took up residence in the downstairs quarters. The other, an older lady with a much fuller figure and greying hair became assigned to the assistant homemother's residence on the up-stairs landing. "Brown!, I would like you to take over the cornet section. I know you can do it. How about it?" How could I refuse this request from the bandmaster himself. The question I suspected,was more a challenge and I had the dis-tinct feeling that my reply was supposed to include the word 'yes'. It appeared that the lead trumpet player was due for discharge some time around Easter and having no immediate re placement meant recruiting someone who in his opinion had a natural ear for music. Looking back,I wish I had possessed the courage to stand up to Mr Dillion and refuse any change of instrument. Instead,my "yes sir," and "thankyou sir" had been just a gesture to please him and promote my own ego. "To play the bugle," so I was informed by another bandboy, "you have to start at a young age,because your lips have to adapt to the constant pressure of the mouthpiece." After a-bout eighteen months of trying to become the world's leading trumpeter I knew my future as a bandsman had suffered a set-back. However,there was a good side to this promotion in as much,as well as receiving recognition as the leading trumpet player,I also took over the duties of 'bugler boy'. I never imagined in my wildest dreams that one day I would succeed in becoming the Home's Bugler,and yet here I was,playing to the whole community,the 'reveille' for morning assembly and 'last post' for the evening lights-out. Unknown to me until a much later date was another bonus,when I found out that I would be eligible to earn two shillings and sixpence for my bugler services during the armistice Sunday parade.

The petrified landscape of the long winter was at last beginning to show signs of seasonal change and Styal,in its slow and gradual process of wakening from its long slumber began to shed its white overcoat. If,as Mr Lyle had suggested,the winter had been the hardest and snowiest for decades, then Springtime,when it arrived,must surely have been the wettest in memory. Gone now,were the frozen streams of the Bollin and Dean,only to be replaced by a swiftly flowing current of dark swirling mud-like soup. The rising river levels were becoming a great concern to the Homes superintendent and it came as no surprise when he issued a warning against venturing too close to the river. Attracted to the flooded valley and swollen rivers,the older boys of the colony became more adventurous in their leisure time and true to form,a mishap occurred in which my friend Wooksie had to be rescued from a life threatening situation. Following this incident,a total ban against playing anywhere near the river was issued, and in order to view the effects of the flooding,it became necessary to walk all the way down Stanneylands Road to the railway arches. During this period of restraint a rumour began to infiltrate the colony which caused a great excitement amongst the children especially the older ones,who wanted to see for themselves the extent of the reputed sea of water in the Bollin Valley. Having completed the Saturday morning job requirements,the gang of boys,myself included,made a beeline for the meeting place at the foot of Twinney's Brow near to the bomb crater. True to the report,the river Bollin had in deed become a lake and the sight of so much water covering the once green meadows was just unbelievable. Skirting the roadside in the direction of Wilmslow,it was possible to see the extent of flooding in the Carrs Wood and where there had been a river there was now just one huge expanse of surging overflow. In my minds eye I could still picture the contour of the riverbank and the lazy-like meanderings of a glistening shallow stream,a brief memory which quickly disappeared under the immense volume and depth of flood water. Two weeks after this episode the customary Sunday walk through the National Trust became reinstated by the Boss who confirmed the safety aspect. Walking in formation along the banks of the Bollin was one of the more exciting walks,depending on which way you looked at it. To the older and more adventurous boys the highlight came when a small section of the river near to Quarry Bank Mill appeared on the horizon. Known locally as the 'swinging bridge',this obstacle,viewed with a dare and bravado by the senior boys,was also an obstacle of fear for the girls and smaller children. Resembling a rope ladder held together by steel cable and slats of wooden flooring,it was stretched across the high banking on either side of the river and secured by strong looking ground pegs. Holding on to the steel cable for support whilst avoiding the gaps between each footstep needed a certain amount of concentration especially if you were affected by height and nerves. On the other hand,there were times,as previously experienced in my own childhood,when the crossing had been an absolute nightmare. This frightening episode only occurred when the leading column was spearheaded by the older boys who,from their hiding place behind the bushes,would swing the cable bridge from side to side. If you were caught in the middle of the gangway during the crossing,the fear would sometimes turn to terror as you viewed the fast flowing river from what seemed a great height.

In the year 1947,I fell in love for the very first time. She was about my age,about my height and in my opinion, nicely shaped and fairly good looking. She didn't know that I had a crush on her and because of my shyness,probably never would. She lived in the home almost opposite to mine and whenever the opportunity arose,such as the lighted bedroom shining in the dark evenings, I would gaze from behind my window blind and hope for a glimpse of her outline. She had a nice complexion and nice shiny hair which was kept off her face with the aid of a shiny brown hairslide. "I know, I'll save my pocket money from my potato picking earnings and go to Woolworths in Wilmslow to buy her a new slide." This idea, just one of many,filtered through my mind in an attempt to find a way to bring us into contact. "There's always the pictures on a Friday night,"I mused. "This wouldn't work either, because the girls were always separated from the boys and sat at a distance on the other side of the aisle. Regrettably, at other times,she was always part of a group and always engaged in some silly game on the playing field,be it skipping routines to a chorus line or bouncing a ball against a wall. Determined to find a way of bringing us together I concluded that the best three possibilities were; a chance meeting in the woods on Saturday,a casual encounter on the playing area near the church,or,if ever I could afford it,an invitation to the Rex pictures in Wilmslow. There was,one other solution,if I had the nerve for it,and that was a love letter. The idea of writing down my feelings and baring my heart seemed to be just the answer I was looking for and thus having deliberated,the next important step would be to buy a notepad and begin my composition. Taking up this enjoyable task with a view to making an impression with my literary knowhow seemed an easy option but after several days and weeks of unfinished practice letters,I regretted my decision. Whether out of desperation,knowing that the opportunity would pass me by unless I made a move,I suddenly discovered the courage I had been looking for. Anxiously,I marched to school on a day just prior to the Easter holidays,a day which with any luck,should present the right opportunity for me to slip the lovingly worded note into her gymslip pocket. Being Easter, meant an extention to the morning assembly for the purpose of an Easter celebration and knowing that we would be crossing paths before departing to the classroom,was going to present the appropiate setting. As usual,the service dragged on and on and my anxiety increased with every repetitive ren

-dering of the Easter hymns. Walking back to the stage for his final address,Smiggy paused to pick up a piece of paper which he shuffled amongst his music sheets before mounting the steps. "Before concluding today's assembly,I want your attention." Smiggy's manner,as he spoke these words,became more ominous by the second as he held aloft a piece of paper "Somebody has been using school notepaper to write obscene messages. This will not be tolerated in this school. I want the author of - "I love you, guess who?" to see me outside my office immediately after dismissal." During the ensuing stifled giggling by the older children,my face coloured up and not wishing to draw attention to my predicament,I too be -gan to join in the muffled laughter. In panic,I felt inside my shirt in the faint hope that maybe somebody else had also written a similar note. "Thank goodness I didn't write down any names. At least,it wont be traced back to me. And thats another thing. I didn't use school notepaper. Admittedly it was a cheap lined paper which resembled the school writing-book paper." During the confusion of hidden glances and hi-larity,my disposition like my red face,had returned to more normal levels and such was my regained confidence,I too ad-opted the 'wonder who it was?'nonchalant attitude of all the other classmates. Secretly,I breathed an inward sigh of re-lief and reflected on what at best,might have made me into a laughing stock for the whole school. At worst,I might have suffered the unthinkable fate of ending up outside Smiggy's office.

CHAPTER NINE

A few months prior to my thirteenth birthday I experienced a feeling of being grown-up,and as each day and week nudged me further into my teens,the sensation of assuredness grew more positive. Accordingly,the Home's work quota, a system which defined a job of work commensurate with age and birthday,instituted a new ranking to my status and seniority. In this atmosphere of eased tensions my confidence began to rise above the normal levels of expectation,inspiring thoughts of new and unconquered horizons. Such was my enthusiasm for a better future,the mere thought of clasping hold a girls hand in the woods became brushed aside in the surging boldness of a ripening maturity. Added to this wave of exuberance were the "prospects" according to Thomas Lyle, "of a beautifully hot summer which,more often than not,followed a bad winter." "Just a few more weeks at school,and then,.." Thoughts of a summer holiday filled with all sorts of adventure became the incentive to tolerate the remainder of what seemed an eternity in the never ending cycle of 'work and school'- 'school and work'routines. If my memory served me correctly, it was at this juncture and by a cruel twist of fate,that the assistant home mother Miss Royden,took a temporary leave of her duties,thus creating an opening for her replacement, a Miss Thomalis. With an immediate impact,the new assistant began her debut at the teatime assembly by announcing a new code of disciplinary measures. Her jet black hair,tied skilfully on the top of her head,not only accentuated her height,but emphasised the length of a hook shaped nose on a long stern face. The concluding words which referred to the"benefits for good behaviour" and "punishment for naughty boys," settled on an audience already subdued by a fear of a new and un -known quantity. On the face of it,her warning about behaviour was not in itself anything to worry about,as this type of authority was food and drink so far as I was concerned. However, there was an underlying element of fear behind her threat,and much to my annoyance,especially in view of my pre -sent relaxed mood,I became peturbed by a strange feeling of uneasiness. Ten days,or there abouts,was all it took before Miss Thomalis stamped her ruling on my night-time habit,and executing it the way she did,was sufficient proof of my suspicions concerning her character. A few introductory clouts across the side of my head was the begining of what was to be,a determined effort once and for all time,to put a stop to my nocturnal habit. "I shall cure you of this despicable carry on if it's the last thing I do." Reflecting on this outburst,caused me to think more seriously about my predicament and I became convinced that had she been informed of my desease,she would have been more understanding.This obser -vation,was probably a reaction to a situation which threatened to turn into a major dilemma and my hope,was for someone to intervene on my behalf. "This,is what you will wear when you go to bed tonight. It will wake you when you need to go the toilet, and don't you dare,let me down." At first sight of the contraption, I failed completely to understand how a long piece of string threaded with wooden bob -bins,could create such magical powers. "I shall be checking to see if you are wearing it properly when I do my rounds to

-night" she continued,as she went on to demonstrate the correct method of application. Apprehensively,with the gadget firmly secured around my back and chest,I settled down uncomfortably for the long night ahead and,for the miraculous remedy that had been assured so long as I played my part. "What if it doesn't work? What if the string snaps? What if,....?" These and many other questions floated in and out of my mind as I twisted and turned in anxiousness,but in the background to all this turmoil there was one misgiving which surfaced like an ominous foreboding,that of reprisal in case of failure. Whether from a reaction to the wooden obstacles digging into me,or a fear of the unknown consequences yet to come about,my nightmare,the familiar one which always depicted me falling from the sky,took an unexpected turn for the worse as suffocation and death became imminent. Waking suddenly from the ordeal brought an instant sigh of relief and after a reassured gaze in the direction of the silhouetted dormitory companions and a drowsy acknowledgement that all was well, returned to my uncomfortable lying position and to a deep slumber. Whack! A resounding succession of clouts a-cross my legs in the early morning light caused me to jump up in fear and half asleep and half in two minds as to what was happening,I saw Miss Thomalis with a slipper in one hand and my discarded bedding in the other. As she continued to reign down,blow after blow,I stumbled over the side of the bed and crawled under the other bedsteads,banging my head in the process. "I'll teach you. I'll teach you not to disobey me" she said,as I scampered down the corridor in escape.

When she did finally catch up with me downstairs,I was cornered in the pantry,where a few more blows were delivered before the order to wash and dress and,.."start by carrying a coal bucket to the outside shed and bring it back full." I could have told her that she was wasting her time in her attempts to find a cure for my noctesis disease,or whatever it was. My instincts over the years had convinced me that there was nothing anybody could do for me and all the good hidings in the world were of no avail. Several days and another succession of experimenting seemed to be enough to con -vince the homemother that her so-called cure and physical abuse was proving futile. "It's attention seeking, that's what it is, attention seeking. Well it wont work on me." These remarks became hurtful,even to the point of making me feel guilty. There had been a time,admittedly,when in retro -spect I had sought attention,but in a very different way and in very different circumstances. My mind slipped back to Miss Chedley's reign and I recaptured the period when for varying reasons,I would bang my head purposely against the solid walls in order to make a bump or even a nasty bruise. That way,I knew that I would be taken into the kitchen and sat on the table and recieve a tender massage from butter coated fingers and a sympathetic hearing of my 'accident'. "You're not going to defy me and get away with it." Snatched from my momentary retreat,I cowered beneath the threatening expanse of starched uniform as Miss Thomalis explained her new plan of action. "From now on,when you go to the laundry you will walk in the middle of the avenue and,you will carry your soiled bed sheets on the top of your head."

That first morning of my new punishment will torment me for years and years to come as I recalled the absolute dread of stepping out of the doorway and into the mainstream avenue leading down to the laundry. My only compensation came in the knowledge that the two homes opposite and the one which was immediately on the left, were occupied by boys and not, girls. As much as I hated recieving punishment,I wished on this occasion,that she had given me a good hiding,or another form of punishment; anything,which would have prevented this loss of dignity. With the threat of "I shall be keeping my eyes on you" ringing in my ears,I felt as if my secret had suddenly become exposed to the whole world and that the eyes of everyone in the colony were peering down on me. Just a week of this public torture was all it took,and suddenly,out of nowhere,the word escape flashed through my mind,telling me that my time had come. To escape from this rotten prison was now the number one priority and whatever the cost,I wouldn't stay in this dump any longer. It wasn't how I had planned to run away,and given the choice I would have preferred a hot summer's day with a well planned itinerary. Recalling the tale told by Amos Lyle of the old Styal hermit who used to live in the cave near to the Quarry Bank mill, I at once knew the whereabouts of my future destiny. "Strange, how after eleven years in the institution,I realized that apart from the immediate vicinity,I was a stranger in a world whose horizons stretched beyond the limits and boundaries of Styal and Wilmslow. "I had to make the Quarry Bank cave my objective; I just didn't know where else to go." This muttered announcement of my intentions became swamped under the deluge of memory jigsaw pieces as I tried to focus on a plan of action centered on the Bollin location of Quarry Bank. Somewhere at the back of my mind was a faint memory of a red sandstone cliff near to the river,a place I had once observed during a Sunday-walk routine. Knowing that a few people still worked at the mill became a major concern,even though I was certain that the density of trees and shrubs around an area near the cave offered good camouflage. It was exactly two days before the weekend,and the choice as I saw it,was to make my escape today,or tomorrow. "Then again, Saturday would be a far better option,and the opportunities would be better placed,especially after the morning work routines." My thoughts,especially about the decision to nominate Saturday,proved to be the right one,especially now that I had got my pocket money of threepence and,another sixpence from my hiding place. Armed with the bottle of dandelion and burdock and a pocket full of sweets and chocolate,I turned out of Station road and into Altrincham road,full of confidence and secure in the knowledge that I wouldn't starve. My original plan had been to start the journey at Bluebell woods,and to then follow the Bollin to my destination. However,it then occurred to me that by walking through Styal village,a route much shorter,I would be able to accumulate more spare time in which to build a den. "If anyone asks me, I've come to watch the cricket match on the village green." This, just one in a line of excuses I was going to offer,to explain my presence in the village, soon became forgotten when the empty cricket field came into view. "I'll think of some other excuse. As long as PC.Waite doesn't come past on his bicycle before I reach the path leading to Norcliffe, I shall be safe." The far side of the village was soon reached, and all that remained was to locate the route which bypassed the mill and find the path which led to Morley Green. I had never taken this route before now but my sixth sense told me that this was the location which Amos Lyle had often mentioned in his references to the Greg's hierarchy. According to one of his stories of the local village life, the very grass I was now trampling underfoot was the same long grass that used to wet the legs of the girls who trekked through the meadows in the early hours, prior to clocking-on at Greg's Mill. The other two clues which gave assurance to my whereabouts was the ivy covered chimney of the mill, and the bridge over the river, both, sure signs that I was nearing the Styal/Wilmslow border that Amos Lyle had talked of. The 'No trespassing' sign situated at the entrance to the meadow at the top of the steep pathway would normally be a deterrent closely observed, but in my present strong mood of defiance and my attitude toward any form of authority, breaching the hedgerows proved to be both effortless and fearless. Inspired by my success, and my journey almost complete, I set off across the field in search of the cliff which, if my reckoning was right, lay just on the horizon beyond the clump of woodland. About halfway across the meadow, the herd of cows which at first sight had seemed very distant, suddenly began closing in on my intended route, and fear,especially of those big horns and imaginary bulls, gripped me so hard that I became terrified. In panic,I made a quick dash into the bushes and scrub,seeking refuge from a mental picture of stampeding animals on the rampage. Whilst regaining my composure and waiting for my heartbeats to slow down I began to make a mental note of my bearings hoping for a clue which would indicate whether I was anywhere near the location of the cave. "If I can find the weir,then I'm almost there." Knowing that the cave lay adjacent to the race was reassuring,especially since I could now not only hear a sound of running water,but actually see the river meandering along the valley below. "What if I slip and hurtle down the embankment into the river? Or,what if I stumble on the rock face above the cave and fall onto some jagged boulders?" Both these fears proved to be very real as I made my way to the river level and finally,with a surface coating of soil, stains and scratches,I proudly emerged to stake my claim on a stretch of the National Trust I deemed to be my own. What confronted me as I looked up at the rock face was not just one cave,but two,almost side by side. Set in the hillside like a pair of eyes,with their outer features covered by a mass of intertwined tree roots,I remembered thinking that Mr Lyle hadn't mentioned there being two caves. Undecided on which cave was the 'old hermit' cave,I surmised that the upper cavern containing machinery parts was probably uninhabit-able and therefore I should settle for the smaller ground-level one,even if there was water in it. Having climbed the boulders to the upper level and to a suitable spot away from prying eyes,I settled down to enjoy,for the first time in my life,a feeling of absolute freedom. Breathing in the fragrance of nature and tasting the success of independence was not only a prescription for the contentment now overtaking my senses,but also the reason for my overall feeling of complete surrender. Where I was going to sleep for the night or where I was going to obtain my next square meal,was of no consequence as I languished in my achievement and new found confidence,a combination which suggested that I could now do "what I want,when I want." "I wish Oakbob and Wooksie were here to share in the adventure. We could build a really big den and light a fire and catch some fishes." Looking down at my boots and observing my muddied appearance confirmed my decision in wearing my corduroy trousers and jacket,and it was reassuring to know that come the evening,I would be prepared for the elements and the first shivers of nightfall. "Before planning my next move,I'll eat my chocolate,have a rest,and then decide." Whether from the excitement and activity, or because of the effects of having a gentle running stream running pass the front door,so to speak, a peace and tranquility descended on me,causing time to become meaningless. Wakening suddenly in the evening dusk,and reacting to a strangely cold environment,I shivered my way to the cave entrance,stumbling from my temporary home into a darkened ex -terior of hostile surroundings. The sudden change in circumstances was dramatic to say the least,as I viewed the deep swirling murkiness of the river and compared it with the shimmering twinkling flow in the late afternoon sun. A new kind of fear,magnified by the darkness and unfamiliar surroundings,began to take over my imagination and suddenly, I was seeing myself floating out of the cave on a bed of tree branches,which disintegrated as it sped over the waterfall. My bravado at the onset of the adventure was now evaporating by the minute as each shadow grew darker and each strange woodland noise grew louder. The fast approaching night-time and the dread of the unknown was enough to convince me that not only had I made a bad decision and couldn't carry it out, but also that I should make a dash for it before it was too late. More from panic than anything else,I stumbled blindly through the woods and reached the area of Styal village near to the Wesleyan chapel in what must have been a record time. By the time I had arrived at the meadow twixt Farm Fold and Bailey's Farm,I realized that it would be impossible for me to attempt to walk through the gates of the colony. A fear of the inevitable reprisal that had accompanied my retreat for most of the return journey,had now convinced me that it would not only be foolish to give myself up,but also that I should look elsewhere for alternate accommodation. "In any case,tomorrow was Sunday,and with everyone being at church, there would be less chance of being apprehended and punished should I decide to surrender." Having settled my mind, the next step was to find a place to sleep and some food to ease the gnawing hunger and with food uppermost in my thoughts, I made a quick dash across the main road into the farmyard of Park's Farm where,from previous visits,I had become familiar with where the sacks of cow chocolate were stored. Having had my fill,I then crept into the barn,thankful that my intrusion hadn't woken the dogs or the geese and more than grateful for the warm bed of straw. Submitting to the natural forces of nature,I drifted into a deep sleep which, owing to my subconscious,became very disturbed with threats and reprisals for running away and stealing cow chocolate. Waking up to a whole bedlam of noise in a farmyard that seemed to explode with early dawn,not only jolted me into realizing the gravity of my situation but triggered a panic and confusion which frightened me to death. Aware that the dog was now in the yard,free of its chain,and that other animals including the bull,were a part of the noisy melee,I forced the window open and jumped quickly down onto the allotment which bordered the rear of the farm and the Open Air School. The woods behind the hospital,my only salvation,were reached in double quick time and it was now a matter of deciding on the next move;another attempt in another direction,possibly Handforth, or,give myself up. The quietness of the early morning felt eerie,even to the point of feeling totally isolated from the rest of civilization. "I wonder what they're doing at this moment? I wonder what time it is? I wonder if they've gone to church yet? I wonder if the police are still searching for me?" My final thoughts on the matter and my ultimate decision were based on my increasing hunger and thirst and a yearning to be back with my pals. Theorising that the longer I stayed absent,the worse the punishment,I concluded that the best time to walk through the gates to give myself up to the Superintendant,would be when everyone was attending the church service, that way, I might receive some sympathy from the assistant House Keeper and maybe, something to eat. On reflection, this decision proved to be one of my better ones in view of the fact that not only did I receive the tea and sympathy as hoped for, but so too did I mysteriously escape a physical good hiding. The only upset during the ensuing interrogation between me, the village policeman, and the Boss, was when threatened in no uncertain manner, of my transfer to a remand home at Mobberley, should I offend again.

From initial reactions, it appeared as though I had won over the system to my side of the story, and judging by the non - aggressive attitude from the house mother, a peaceful conclusion seemed to have been achieved to the satisfaction of all. In fact, when looking back on the whole affair, things did improve generally for some time after, but both Miss Thomalis and myself were under no illusions about the ill feeling between us and that it would only be a matter of time before the fragile truce became severed. As it stood, there was an uneasy intermission where I was ahead on points and the continuity was based on the theme of 'unfinished business'. Weeks, rather than days, was the length of time it took for a clash of opposite personalities to erupt and when it did, on a day during the summer holidays, it was all down to a normal something and nothing incident. If my memory serves me correct, it occurred on a Saturday morning when the completed work rotas were due to be inspected, and Miss Thomalis giving instructions for me to "do it all again". My cool defiance in answering back, and my refusal to do the job of work for a

second time, was to become the final straw which broke the camel's back. Painstakingly,that very morning,I had methodically red-leaded the floors of the pantry and all the corridor area near to the house entrance door, and so far as I was concerned,it was one of my better performances. Snapping uncontrollably,she dragged me by the hair into the kitchen, and holding me down across the table,laid into me with whatever implement she could lay her hands on. Even to this day I have no idea what the weapon was that was administered across my back,but whatever it was,the effects lasted for days if not weeks,causing discomfort when ever I came into physical contact. My severely bruised pride was another matter, and once again I knew that the system and Miss Thomalis,had won the day,leaving me not only heart broken and despondent but painfully aware that submission and surrender was going to be the only way for future peaceful co-existence. Exactly one week from the time of that good hiding and when queuing up for my Saturday pocket money with all the other children, a gentle tap on my shoulder by no lesser person than Matron, caused my face to redden with guilt at the thought of more trouble. "Jimmy Brown,Mrs Huggins wants you in her office after the pocket money and sweets have been given out." Inwardly,my heart missed a beat at the prospect of another imminent fate but as I analysed the situation and deemed the Matron's pronouncement to be more of a request as opposed to an order,I deemed the matter to be of a trivial nature.
"Come in, Brown." So far,so good,were my thoughts as Matron ushered me into the office,her voice still without emotion.

Both the Boss and his wife were sat at the desk as I entered the room and cutting short their conversation,Mrs Huggins re -quested me to step forward and stand in front of her. "Now then,Jimmy Brown, I want you to take off your shirt and face the wall behind you." "Oh no!, I'm going to be in trouble for answering back at the home mother." As I began to sur- mise my fate,a silence that seemed to go on forever,settled like an invisible blanket on the room and its occupants. A gentle prodding to various parts of my back and shoulders be -came the prelude to the next stage of events, and breaking the silence,a voice said; "does this hurt when I touch you?" My intuition was begining to imply that all was not well for Miss Thomalis and that as a result of this interview,I would pay with many more good hidings,being her way of getting her own back. The whispering and prodding continued until Mrs Huggins finally instructed me to put my shirt back on and ex -plain in full,why I had been beaten black and blue. Whether my version was accepted as being the right one, or whether the home mother had been adjudged as being cruel and without mercy,was of little consequence since I never saw or heard of her again,ever. From that very day in the Superintendants office,she disappeared from the Homes without trace.

For anyone who has experienced the joys of waking up in the countryside environment where clean air,the smell of nature, and early morning sunshine contribute to that spiritual and mental awareness, then it is they who will understand the ex -pression; 'being at peace with nature and all mankind'. Such a day,the only one in all my life I can recall,occurred some weeks before my thirteenth birthday. Specifically,I rememb-ered waking up feeling completely relaxed and devoid of any of the tensions that I normally faced. It was as if I'd awake-ned from a long winter hibernation and opened my eyes to a beautifully sunny outlook on the first day of Spring. My ex-citement and happiness became briefly interrupted as I com-pared my circumstances with that of a chrysalis of a moth, who's transformation into a butterfly heralded not only a se-verance from it's past,but signalled a new life and a new future. That I was now cured of my disease was a certainty which needed no second opinion or,verification. Leaving be-hind the shackles of a lifetime's trauma,I walked away from the dormitory with a smile and a confidence which proclaimed to the world that I was free at last. "I'm cured. The mir-acle I've always prayed for,has happened." The desire to re-veal my new identity to the whole community and to celebra-te my conversion became suddenly stopped in its tracks as I realised the impossiblity. In view of the personal nature of the subject,any celebrating would have to be completely private. It all seemed such a shame that my achievement, a fulfilment that cried out for some kind of recognition,shou-ld be extinguished without trace.

Not only did my spirits spiral in anticipation of the new re-vitalised Jimmy Brown,but so too was there an upsurge in confidence relating to new challenges and new teenage confr-ontations. It was about this period in my life that some-thing began to take place;something to do with emotions. I couldn't put a name to this new phenomenon but I was becoming increasingly aware of a distraction in my normal every-day outlook which, not only directed my attentions away from cowboys,comics and catapaults,but channelled my curiosity to -wards the fascination of the female sex. My affections had deserted the girl in the home opposite mine and were now en-trusted to another who lived in 'A' Home. We had already ex -changed a brief kiss whilst in the sunken gardens opposite the Lodge,and the memory of her wet lingering lips and the fragrance of carbolic soap in her hair,was sufficient to add even more inspiration to my dreams and fantasies. "Soon, it will be bonfire night,and when all the fireworks and treacle toffee have come to an end, I'll ask her to slip away into the woods." This plan of action,if successful, and if my daring attitude held firm, could result in my first ever con -frontation,and not only would I then steal more than just one kiss,but hopefully encounter an exciting close contact with her large rounded contours. "A visitor for Jimmy Brown". Once again this unfamiliar call to the Lodge summoned me to attend a 'visit' by my sister Sylvia,and once again the wash and change routine became a necessary part of the process be -fore being allowed my appointment. "I hope she's got me a present,or something for my coming birthday?" My mind wand-ered momentarily to the previous visit,and just as I began to recall the nicer aspects of that family get together,I es -pied the outlines of Vera and Sylvia standing in front of the gates. I had never seen Vera dressed up before now. In fact, I had never seen any of the other Styal Homes girls wearing that uniform. My first reaction was to compare her long jacket and white cotton neck scarf with that of a grown woman especially since that was how she appeared as I neared the Lodge. Vera,was the first to run towards me as I hesitated,and it was obvious that there was something very different about her. "Jimmy, I've left the Homes, I've gone to work in Manchester and live not far from Sylvia." There was a big smile on her face and an excitement in her manner that spelled happiness and enthusiasm. There was also a new kind of matronly fussiness about her which suggested that she was no longer the schoolgirl of yesterday,but rather,a grown-up lady like Sylvia. "I wonder why I wasn't told she had left?" The last time I had seen Vera was at the swimming gala when I had swanked because my sister had won the 'best diving' competition. "Funny how people spent years and years living in the colony and then disappeared one day without a trace." This,had always been a mystery to me,but now that my sister had become one of those vanishing children,I felt annoyed with the authorities for not telling me. Turning my attention to Sylvia,I shyly gazed at her smiling face as she said; "How are you Jimmy?" Again,as happened on the last occasion, there was that same feeling of being looked on by an angel in the guise of a human being,wearing beautifully tailored clothes and always with that saintly smile. That she was a good looking girl,was a fact still borne out by some of the older boys of the Homes,who each claimed that Sylvia Brown had been "their" girl friend. Smiling coyly as they both gave me a hug,I looked in every direction to make sure that I was not being observed. "Would you like to go to the pictures in Wilmslow,Jimmy?" I quickly replied "yes" to this suggestion hoping that it would accelerate the formalities,because out of the corner of my eye, I'd spotted the big parcel that Sylvia had placed on the benchseat. "This is a present for your birthday,Jimmy. We've brought it early,so that you can have lots of use before the winter. Go on, open it,and let's see what you think about it." Shyly, my face red from the embarrassment of so much attention, I undid the the paper to reveal a beautiful pair of chromium plated roller skates. I was completely lost for words. They were without a shadow of a doubt,the bestist present I had ever had in my whole life and I was well aware that not only was I the only boy in the colony to possess a pair of skates,but also that I would now be the envy of every other child. "I hope they don't get taken off me until I'm older,or put into the open lockers of the playroom where they'll get pinched." The full impact of the gift,which I was convinced had cost Sylvia and Vera lots of money,was not felt until later in the month when I had the opportunity to examine in detail the high quality of the wheel bearings. Meanwhile,with gratefulness still pouring from me,we all set off down Twinney's Brow to walk through the Carrs woods to the Rex,where,I had been informed, they were showing their first ever picture incorporating the new technicolour system. On reflection,that 'visiting day' and the events which helped to turn it into such a lasting memory,will forever be synonymous with a family gathering,when, for the first time,I experienced a closeness and a feeling of belonging. By the time of my sisters departure at the gates, late in the afternoon, I couldn't help but dwell on the fact that they were leaving me behind, and that I was now the last of the 'Brown's' of the Styal Orphanage. Following the tears and the farewells and a promise to Vera that I would be good, I reciprocated their hand waving until they reached the boundary of Park's Farm when, at that point, I retreated inside the gates of my home and into my own world of secure anxieties. At bedtime that same night, I relived the events of my 'visit', and with the accompaniment of the musical chorus of "Zip-a-de-doo-dah" (the musical film of that afternoon) still uppermost in my mind, I marvelled, along with many other things, at how grown-up Vera had become, and at her transformation from a schoolgirl into a handsome lady. During the brief period when that kind man had taken our photograph near Wilmslow station, I had felt very proud of being related to two such beautiful ladies and in spite of my shyness, I had actually attempted to link them from behind.

Styal homes.

C H A P T E R T E N

Whether from being a popular figure at school or in recognition of a long service record or,just being next in line for some kind of promotion, the new Autumn term brought with it, enough support to claim the title of 'school prefect', a new status that I was convinced would excuse me any more punishment from Smiggy. Joining my new term classmates and taking my place at the front of the class,a requirement for any new graduate,became more of an ordeal in view of the seemingly comical appearance portrayed by the loose fitting prefects jacket hanging from my shoulders. Probably,as an initiation, or some kind of welcoming,a missile,more than likely a bent paper clip fired from an elastic band,landed on the back of my neck as the lessons got under way. Turning round to pull a face at the culprit whilst screwing up a ball of paper to throw in his direction,I ducked my head to avoid his next volley. What happened next could only be described as a very tragic turn of events,and yet,when bringing this episode to mind,I can only laugh at what to me was the hilarious begining of a farce that went sadly wrong. Like mine and everyone else's desk,each contained a supply of pencils,pens,ink and blotting and writing paper,not to mention the text books and customary twelve-inch ruler. Quickly diverting my attention to the class in progress and assuming that because of the lesson,no further interruption would take place,I began to concentrate on the importance of what the teacher was trying to convey. In total disbelief,my gaze became riveted to a black blob of wet ink that was slowly running down the wall in front of me. Throughout the school,the smell of new paint was a reminder that the school interior had undergone a major refurbishment during its holiday closure and that its shiny cream and green walls were evidence of the highest standard of workmanship. It became obvious from the growing silence that the blob had been spotted by others in the room and just as the stain became more conspicuous in its trickle of blackening doom,so too did the contrasting lighter colour of emulsion become much lighter. By this time,the rest of the class had begun to share in what was the funny side of the prank and as I turned round to pinpoint the offender, I noticed the ink stained hands trying fervently to wipe clean an ink stained ruler. Aware of the seriousness of the situation and under no illusions as to why the atmosphere had suddenly become still and quiet,the whole of the class watch -ed in suspense as the teacher took one look at the stained wall,then glanced straight faced at the culprit,who's guilt had been made obvious by the stares from other classmates, and then,without a word to anyone,walked out of the door and in the direction of Smiggy's office. At that point,and with a heartfelt sympathy that recognized the ominous signs of an imminent punishment,I commiserated in joint fear at what the headmaster's reaction might be. Not daring to look around for fear of repercussions,I tried to imagine what must have been going through his mind in the continuing silence. He too was called Jimmy,and although not the eldest amongst his brothers and sisters,his trademark as a likeable joker and a carefree bounder earned him a great deal of popularity with the majority of his age group. Even he must have concluded that a punishment of some kind was impending and even more so considering the unusual manner in which the teacher had left the room. Presumably,the teacher's mission was to inform Mr Smith personally of the magnitude of the offence and to hasten his appearance on the scene. To the relief of myself and no doubt the majority of the class,a temporary recess emerged by way of a remark shouted by someone on the back row. "Put some books down the back of yer trousers, Jimmy." As one or two more added their advice and comments, I myself couldn't resist the urge to enter into the spirit of the interlude but instead of joining in any chorus,I chose instead to focus on Jimmy's last moments before the projectile left its launch. Smiling to myself,I projected the image of cheeky faced Jimmy tearing off a piece of blotting paper and then immersing it in the inkwell prior to aiming it at the back of my head from the tip of the wooden ruler. The black look on Smiggy's face as he entered the room and the size of the stick held in his hand,was enough to spread fear to every member of the class. Looking up to inspect the blob,which by now had grown a few more tentacles,he then turned to face what could only be described as a petrified audience of attentive upright pupils. "What has occurred in this classroom today,is no more than downright hooliganism. A lot of time and money has been spent by the Manchester authorities in maintaining this building just for you, and if you think you can deface the walls and get away with it, you are sadly mistaken." Diverting his stare from the rest of the class,he then turned to the guilty boy and said;"Come to the front,Needham, I'm going to teach you a lesson you will never forget." The wrath of Smiggy's anger was reflected almost immediately as he rapped Jimmy's hand from underneath, in an effort to get him to hold his outstretched arms as high as possible. I had never seen a punishment being given in the classroom before,and that in itself should have told me how the headmaster viewed the incident and why he was about to set an example to the rest of the school. True to his character,,Jimmy's stubborness held firm throughout the punishment and by the time the sixth stroke had been dealt, the defiant attitude had held firm and eclipsed what should have been a deluge of tears. As Smiggy made his exit, the whole class gave a sympathetic acknowledgement to Jimmy's bravery knowing that in spite of his seemingly courageous at-titude,the physical assault must have produced some symptom of pain in one way of another. From first hand experience,I knew the kind of excrutiating agony that lingered long after the punishment had ceased and I sympathised with Jimmy as he tried to relieve the pain by tuckng his hands underneath his armpits. My concern for Jimmy intensified when I spotted blood stains on the floor, and only when the class had ended was I able to survey the damage to his fingers,which by this time, having been covered in blotting paper,resembled a ball of red papier maché. This incident,now stored away in my mem-ory, was to become synonymous with the game of cricket, for whenever Jimmy's bowling deteriorated during a cricket match he never failed to describe how his finger had been split apart by Smiggy's stick,and how his spin bowling had been affected by the scar that covered the area of the wound.

"Don't you think you should share your skates with somebody else? You can use one skate and let your pals share turns on the other one." This suggestion by Mr Dillion on the fir -st day of trying out my new acquisition,and although not a direct order,was a strong hint that the proposal made good sense and that it would be wise of me to take up his recomm- endation. "Yes sir!" I replied,as I took off the skate att- ached to my left foot and handed it to one of my pals. "It's not fair," I thought to myself. "These are my skates and my inheritance. I shouldn't have to be told what to do with my own possessions." "That's a good lad," said the bandmaster, "now,everyone's happy." The resentment of his interference and my own acceptance of his untimely judgement became an ir -ritation that niggled me for many weeks. "I wonder what my sisters would think if they knew that I had to divide their present between all the other boys?" Unfortunately,this ar- rangement was to last for the duration,until eventually the skates either disappeared or were broken. Ironically, the Superintendant himself,was the very person who brought me to a halt some months later,with the information that skating on one leg was the worst thing I could do,and that by using only one skate,I would end up with one leg a lot longer than the other.

I now had a hobby. Not that I had forsaken my interest in the opposite sex. This,was totally different. It was called Stamp Collecting. My fascination for this subject had come about after seeing an album belonging to one of the apprentice shoemakers who worked in the shoe repair shop. His collection of beautiful postage stamps from all over the world had captivated my attention to such a degree that from that moment,I knew that I would become addicted. Gone now,was my normal desire to spend any spare money on sweets or marbles or any other childish bric-a-brac. Even my treasured catapault had lost its appeal,especially since my last adventure in the woods when I had killed a Blue Tit by mistake and had to bury it out of remorse. With a burning excitement to discover all I could about the rudiments of philately,I began a plan of action that would enable me to compile an album and fill it with collections of stamps from all over the world. Momentarily,I abandoned my Saturday afternoon contact with the girl from 'A' Home as I journeyed to Wilmslow in pursuit of my new found leisure activity. There was a shop there,in Church street,known as Sant's Newsagents,just next door to Clegg's gown shop,and from various sources of information, I had learned of their notoriety as retailers of "the best collection of foreign stamps in the neighbourhood". After several weeks and several major 'swaps' of personal items, I had amassed a sizeable collection of stamps,enough in my opinion,to warrant its classification as being that of a rare collection. Only recently,because of my inability to sleep after the 'lights out' and 'no talking' bedtime ritual,I had devised a wonderful invention to enable me to read comics under the bedclothes. The simple device which gave out enough light to read,consisted of a small flat battery with two met

-al prongs,two long lengths of shiny wire,and a small screw-in torch bulb. With the light from my new contraption,I was now able to transport my imagination across the far oceans as I became more knowledgeable of the vast array of land and countries and,of the political and social trends depicted on an assortment of beautifully coloured stamps.

Of course,I hadn't really relinquished my interest in the opposite sex and if anything,the situation was improving each week,so far as my learning about nature was concerned. Only recently,a new dimension had been added to my bath-time routine,which had transformed it from an everyday dull habitual ablution,into one of the most exciting and new experiences of my whole life. In retrospect,it was probably my first introduction into an adolescent inquisitiveness that has continued ever since,and because of what took place,my yearning for sexual knowledge became heightened almost to fever point. Once a week,usually on a Saturday,it was the tradition for the housemother to supervise the bathing of each individual boy,and to make doubly sure that the ears were cleaned out, the hair properly washed,and the neck scrubbed. There were of course,other obvious parts of the anatomy such as knees, hands and feet that were equally important,but in my case,it was the section around my private parts and buttocks that appeared to recieve the most attention. Maybe it was my fertile imagination or,maybe it was because of the delicate manner in which Miss Miniver's arm brushed ever so gently side to side across my lower front,causing an arousal of unimaginable proportions as her soapy hands explored the crevices.

The bathroom consisted of two large deep baths,one for the housemother and the other for the children. After teatime, on every Saturday evening,the bathing routine comprised of a queue of boys of every age,all lined along the upstairs corridor,and all awaiting their call to go behind the screen to receive a personal scrubbing by the housemother. The very first time that I showed a response to the soapy massage in and around my private parts,I stood there in a state of arrousal,waiting for a slap across my head for being impudent. In absence of any such clout materialising,I continued to ob-serve Miss Miniver's delicate rinsing and sponging and con-cluded that if she didn't mind my display of manhood,then I also,with a certain amount of embarrassment,didn't mind eith-er. I had noticed that whenever Miss Miniver was on bathing duties,she always removed her spectacles,probably due to them either getting wet,or becoming steamed up. This last thought brought a wicked smile to my face as I humorously compared her to a sketch I had seen of Will Hay,who's short sightedness without his pince-nez,caused him to fumble about with his hands to locate whatever it was he had mislaid.
When I had been under the supervision of Miss Chedley,one of her favourite expressions amongst her words of encouragement when woken in the night to use the potty,was;"little Jimmy". "Come on, where's little Jimmy," she used to say,as she fumbled for my little possession. Thoughts of this almost forgotten episode and the comparison with the present situation were sufficient to reward my thoughts with the biggest smile possible as I propelled the obvious 'big Jimmy' to the fore-

front. Apart from the temporary and inconsistent breaks of weekend leave by the home mother,the bath time fantasies con-tinued with every meaningful contact, and I was becoming aware of a new boldness which dared her to view the results of her skill,after using the soap and flannel. Eventually, time ran out on this most provocative,secretive and personal adventure,and where once the fires of imagination had almost burned beyond control,they became extinguished with the implementation of an age old tradition. In other words,I had received a promotion,whereas from now on,I was deemed to be old enough to join the handful of senior boys who were classed as being old enough to bathe themselves. Bathtime,I concluded,would never be the same again,but on the other hand, in view of my new knowledge and experience,there might be a new adventure,especially with the girl who's brother was a pal of mine in 'N' Home. This,another wishful thought,and one which was on par with all the other fantasies,became relegated,knowing full well that firstly,I didn't have the nerve to ask her out,and secondly,I was too shy to allow myself to be seen with a girl.

"Brown!, you've been selected for the Christmas party at the BBC,in Manchester. Report to my office this afternoon for a word with Matron." This inspiring news from the Boss was enough to bring a ray of sunshine to my immediate horizons, especially since dreary old winter was the only future ahead of me,and even that,including Christmas,appeared to be lacking in any new ideas. There was the Christmas partying,of course,and hopefully,I'll be going to the Belle Vue circus.

That party at the BBC in Piccadilly,was a day I shall treasure if only for the memory of those beautiful lumbering red and white trams rumbling along their tracks. The grime on the glass and the high positioning of the windows had prevented a clear view of the city traffic as the Chara made its way into the city,but as soon as my feet touched the cobbled stones and the shiny rail tracks came into focus,I felt as if my dream had at last come true. There was a vibrant feel about Manchester that was like nothing else,and even the awe-some prospect of becoming lost in the big city did little to distract my yearnings to be a part of such an exciting metropolis. "Only a short time to go,and then I'll be able to leave the Styal orphanage and come to live in Manchester" This,my departing thought as I boarded the Chara outside the BBC,was more a reference to the tram system of the city,who's magnetism had manoeuvred my thoughts once again to its overpowering attraction. Having settled into my seat for the re-turn journey,my head still buzzing from all the day's encounters,it was only a matter of moments before I resumed my customary wishing sequence,where,my natural urge was compell-ing me to wish that I would have much rather taken a tram ride in preference to the Christmas party. To be fair, the BBC party in the upstairs room overlooking Piccadilly was,if nothing else,a great treat of cakes and lemonade,and jellies and blancmange. The party,compered by a man and a woman whose names were Violet Carson and Jack Watson,was strangely out of tune to the normal fun and games back at the Homes, and the shyness and quietness of all the boys and girls,almost brought about a premature ending to the programme's al -lotted hour of merrymaking.

When the circus season came around,usually in February,there was a noticeable increase in good behaviour,this,being the second most important highlight in the years' itinerary,next to the summer holiday excursion. This year,I knew for definite that I was eligible to join in this breathtaking experience,and to make doubly certain of my inclusion,I began to include fresh vigour to the hated chores of my everyday life. The good behavioural pattern and the extra impetus became ex -tinguished by the uninspiring monotony,and before very long I began yearning for some kind of alternative adventure. The Christmas bonanza of comic book annuals,especially the Beano, Dandy and Hotspur,had all been read and re-read,and even my most unusual present from my sisters,a kaleidascope,had outlived its impact and had become a 'swap' in exchange for a packet of foriegn stamps. My attention,most probably due to a temporary drought of girl friends,inevitably converged on past intimacies,especially those close contact memories encountered in the bathroom with the housemother. Many's the time I had wished for a resurrection of those warm and intox -icating evenings and many's the time I had regretted my bad luck in being promoted to the senior boys rankings. My fertile and overactive mind,which always appeared to increase in activity after the eight-o-clock lights out had,of late, conceived a new exciting challenge. "If only I could pluck up the courage to carry out this daring enterprise?" The more I thought about it the more convinced I became of my eventual success,should I put it into practice. Having made the all important decision,the day finally arrived,bringing with it,an excitement and anticipation that was almost unb-earable,and because the event was timed for the late evening, the suspense increased with each hour of the approaching dar -kness. The 8-pm 'lights out'eventually arrived as did the short interval that followed before the housemother made her final inspection. All that remained now was try to stay a-wake long enough to observe her final rounds before retire-ment to her quarters. The temptation to nod off on what see -med the longest night of my life,came to a head when my de-termination was rewarded by the clicking of light switches and the patter of footsteps. Keeping my eyes tightly shut in order to feign sleep,I waited for the creaking staircase to advertise her withdrawal from the upstairs of the build-ing knowing that with the final click of her bedroom door, the day's duties had come to an end. "At last!, all I have to do now is wait for about another ten minutes." This,my final thought before mentally preparing myself for the task ahead of me became the sequel to an emotional flurry of ner-ves as I hesitated for some kind of reassurance. "After all, what could be more simple than creeping down the stairs to Miss Miniver's bedroom door and taking a peep through the tiny keyhole?" Calculating that by now,enough time had elap-sed for her to be in the stages of undressing,I cautiously made my way down the stairs,whilst making sure that I avoid-ed the creaking sections of the well worn,polished surface. Gliding silently along the downstairs corridor,I then took up a comfortable position before taking my first peep into the homemother's bedroom. The reward,a revelation of female maturity,was much more than I had hoped for. In the distance Miss Miniver was half way between dressed and undressed and her nudity,from the waist down,was an exhibition I couldn't quite digest. Standing to my feet whilst trying hard to con -tain a turmoil of mixed emotions,I shivered with excitement as I brought to mind what I had just seen. With double quick composure I returned to my kneeling position for a continu- ation of my private peep show. What met my eyes on this oc- casion could only be described as a symbol of all my dreams and imaginations, an angel,without any clothes on. At that very moment of capturing in cameo,the treasure of all treas- ures,an alarm bell sounded in my head as she began walking towards the door. "She must have seen me." I jumped up in a blind panic,convinced that she was about to open the door, and confused and blinded by fright and hysteria,I ran into the adjoining pantry come storeroom where the darkness caus- ed a further crisis. "Crash! Bang! Clatter!" The loud noise of pandemonium errupted as I dislodged hanging pans of every description with my head,whilst my feet displayed an even better accuracy with the buckets and brushes and good- ness knows what. There was only one thing left,and that was to make it back to my bed before she had time to dress. With a distant shout of "who's that?" ringing in my ears,I raced at full speed up the stairs and along the corridor to my bed where I scrambled under the bedclothes and closed my eyes to impersonate sleep. "If only my heartbeats would stop pounding,otherwise,how am I going to feign a deep slumber?" Fortunately,in the few minutes it took for the housemother to regain her composure and emerge from her bedroom in night at -tire,my heavy breathing had subsided to a shallow rythym. As she made her inspection amongst the sleeping corpses of the senior boys bedroom,she stopped at the foot of two other beds before arriving to where I had hidden myself under the bedclothes. Lifting the sheets and shaking me by the shoulders,as she had done with the other two boys,she said:"Brown was that you?" Resisting the temptation to open my eyes, I turned over and pulled the sheet with me. "Jimmy Brown! Was that you downstairs?" This time,I opened my eyes as if disturbed from a deep sleep and mumbled an answer to her question. "Me M'm? No M'm. Wasn't me M'm." Needless to say, that avenue of adventure was never repeated and the one big question which arose from that incident,was whether I was a prime suspect or just one of many others. I was sure that I had given one of my best performances when she had interrogated me that night. "Oh well, at least I can carry on look -ing through the bedroom windows undetected and who knows? If that girl in 'B' Home continues to undress herself standing in front of the windows with the light on and the blinds undrawn,then I might get a glimpse of her figure.

The continuing promise of better things to come,especially where morale was concerned,was demonstrated with the introduction of a radio to each home. In my own case,the talking box was never more appreciated,even if it was limited to one half hour before going to bed,and 'silent night' Mondays', a term used to describe the quiet hour on a Monday evening, when sock darning became a whispered routine,was now almost a pleasant job of work in a more relaxed atmosphere. On the financial side,my savings,hidden away in my secret hiding place,had now reached the amazing total of three shillings, and that,was in some way,due to Mr Dillion recommending me to the Minister of the Styal Wesleyan Church. As a result, I had been awarded the post of 'air blower' at the chapel on every Sunday evening and the reward for pumping air into the church organ was sixpence per service. The military band of the Styal Homes,according to Thomas Lyle,was the backbone of the establishment and had been so,for the past fifty years. Remembering his stories of the numerous bandsmen who,along with their regiments,had travelled all over the world, I became saddened by the rumour that not only was the band about to disintegrate,but that owing to a shortage of recruits and a falling interest in military matters,Mr Dillion was also abdicating. To me personally,this was both good and bad news although my orders for the foreseeable future was to carry on playing the bugle for revellie and last post. Typical of Mr Dillion's personality was the uncertainty of his moods, especially whenever anybody presumed they were in his good books and found themselves on the receiving end of a verbal or physical onslaught. Such had been the case only a few weeks ago when he had caught me unawares trying to imitate one of the comedians I had heard on the newly installed wire-less. Adopting the expression from a particular programme, mainly because it had a nice comfortable ring to it,I began vocalizing the words: "cor,blimey". The hard slap across my face that came out of the blue,together with my wounded pri-de,was proof that I had in some way made a bad choice. His raging verbal assault came to a climax as he pinpointed the reason for his anger. "Don't you ever use those words again Do you know what it means? It's blasphemy. It means, God blind me." I was in no position to deny or argue with him, but because of that incident,I became totally convinced that his leaving would be 'good riddance to bad rubbish'.

The apprehensions which had dogged me for most of the year were in some way due to the fact that come my fourteenth bir-thday,I would have to leave the house I had grown up in and transfer to the 'big boys' home. The deadline for my depart-ure was still some weeks if not months away,but already the nostalgia centred on my early life was begining to have some bearing on what was ahead of me. "One thing, when I'm four-teen,I'll get an increase in pocket money." Thoughts of the one shilling a week,my new entitlement,brought back a memory of a shiny shilling piece which Sylvia had once given me. "On the other hand,if I ask for my pocket money to be paid in pennies and halfpennies,..." In my mind,I began a calcu-lation of all the possibilities within the realms of my new found wealth. "Threepence,could get me a back row seat at the Rex cinema,and if I ask a girl to go with me,that would still leave me with another sixpence. Out of that,I could then buy some packets of foreign stamps and have enough left to buy some sweets and 'pop'." Growing up I decided,was not a bad idea,since the more mature one became,the more the rewards and opportunities,and this year,knowing that at last I would be eligible for the holiday in Abergele,gave an assurance of euphoric proportions. The present everyday life in the Homes however,was still routinely anchored to the hub of the housemother's domain where,the prospects of escaping the gruelling fluctuating work schedules were almost non existent. Saturdays,the one 'playing out' day of the week, never became sanctioned until all the jobs of work had received a pass of merit from either the assistant housemother - whose authority was normally not as strict - or the official house mother. On one particular Saturday,I became resentful and almost mutinous at being ordered to do my mornings' work all over again and my stubborn attitude almost resulted in a major confrontation. As it was,that incident turned out to be the main reason behind an unexpected and very pleasurable ex -perience. My job allocation on the particular Saturday in question,was to wax and polish the upstairs landing corridor, a dreary time consuming process which was performed on hands and knees. Seemingly,Miss Miniver had either been in a bad mood or she had been convinced that I had shirked in my efforts to produce the right amount of shine on the linoleum. With a high pitch tantrum of shouting,and an order to "do it all again after mid-day dinner time", I remembered thinking; "that's the end of my playing out today,by the time I've fin -ished,I'll have missed all the fun down at the Bollin,inclu -ding the planned stone throwing fight against all the Bower gang of Lacey Green". Uttering a string of hateful remarks against the homemother,I set about the task of repolishing, including all the nooks and crannies of every alcove and all the awkward bits in and around every doorway,stopping only to throw another dollop of polish on each section of floor space. Such was the case as I adjusted my kneeling position outside the bathroom doorway and realized that the room was being used. Turning quickly from side to side to make sure I was alone,I peered through the keyhole to observe the head and shoulders of Miss Royden as she sat with her back facing me whilst sitting in the bath. "Of course, Saturday after-noon is when the housemothers have time to themselves and in -dulge in their own pursuits." A renewed mood of excitement suddenly loomed on the horizon as I patiently waited for an indication that she was either going to stand up and face my direction or,just emerge from the bath in all her glory. As it was,her ablutions seemed to take up most of her attention and all I could do in between an occasional flick with the polishing cloth,was to let my fertile imagination reap havoc "What are you doing in front of that doorway?" A shout from Miss Miniver who had completely taken me by surprise as she walked towards me,caused me to panic with terror as I tried desperately to imitate a polishing routine near the doorway. Tapping gently on the bathroom door and receiving the expect -ed confirmation,she then grabbed hold of my ear and yanked me to my feet. "You filthy little boy. What were you doing?" My reply of "yes M'm,no M'm" became completely ignored as she verbally reduced my self esteem to that of a small rat. "For the next four weeks,you will continue to spend your Saturday afternoons polishing the bedroom floors and woe betide if I ever catch you spying through keyholes again." By the time the following Saturday had arrived my resentment of the over -all Styal Homes system of work,work and more work,had errup -ted into a defiant attitude of 'don't care anymore' and it was only the fear of reprisal that prevented a show of mart-yrdom. "I know, I'll take some comics with me, and in be-tween polishing the floors,I'll climb onto a shelf in the clothes cupboard and have a good read." Feeling better al-ready,I abandoned my chore halfway through the afternoon and settled on the top shelf of the storeroom in amongst all the Sunday suits of clothes. With a quick glance through the up -per window of my hideaway,I observed the bathroom on the opposite side of the corridor and was painfully reminded of the reason for being in this predicament. With an inquisi-tiveness that was second nature,I cautiously took a peep at the bathroom window which,because of my elevation,was now at a lower level. In disbelief at what had met my gaze,I quick-ly scampered down from the shelf and ran into the bedroom to resume my polishing. Shaking with an almost uncontrollable excitement,my heartbeat pounding away to an increased rhythm, I mentally explored the scene I had just witnessed of Miss Royden lying completely naked in a bath of soapy water. I just couldn't believe my luck. "I've struck gold." This, and other thoughts were begining to run amok as I reviewed Miss Miniver's punishment and especially the hatred I had be -gun to show her. All of a sudden,as if by a magical wand,I had developed a liking for my Saturday punishment and even a forgiving attitude towards the senior homemother. Not wanting to waste a minute more than was necessary,I made my way back to the top shelf viewing position from where I could ob -serve the rest of Miss Royden's bathing routine. My eyes began to focus on the two glistening mounds protruding above the water and as I became mesmerised by the pulsating rhythm of the two giant globes,I daringly ventured into a wishful fantasy where I,was assisting with the application of the big bar of soap to the body. My fascination at Miss Royden's nudity was almost too much to take in as she continued using the soap to the remaining parts of the body,and only when she became engrossed in the lower regions did my attention divert to the most secretive of secrets,a treasure chest of jewelled knowledge that was far beyond my innocence and understanding. Against all the odds,and a niggling temptation to share the discovery with my pals,the Saturday afternoon flirtation was probably the ultimate amongst my best kept se -crets and not surprisingly,I attempted to misbehave just for the sole purpose of being sentenced to more of the Saturday afternoon punishments of hard labour.

Burning of Manchester's last trams 1949.
Sincere thanks to Ian Yearsley and the Tram Museum at Crich.

C H A P T E R E L E V E N

Such was the impact of my first ever real holiday experience that no matter how simple the episode appeared,nothing could compare with the sheer ecstasy at having been a part of what in my case,was the event of the decade. Looking back,almost as if it were yesterday,I can still taste the salty air of the North Wales coastline where even the faintest breeze exuded an aroma of sea and sand. Abergele,it was generally un -derstood,was a holday resort which contained a number of wooden chalets that catered for the underpriviledged children who,like us,could spend up to two weeks at a time,enjoying the fun,freedom,fresh air,and that greatest attraction of all,the sea. Just along the coast,a mere bus ride away, was another even bigger resort known as Rhyl where,according to heresay,not only had it got the largest sandiest beaches around,but more especially,the biggest fun fair in the world. Speaking for every one of the children,including myself,on the occasion of that memorable visit to Rhyl,all of the sixpenny rides paled into insignificance compared to the one simple device that captivated all the Styal childrens' atten -tion: Bicycles! More to the point,there were two wheel bi -cycles as well as three wheel bicycles which accommodated two people at a time. For most,like myself,riding a bicycle was a lifelong ambition and it was no surprise that almost all the children opted for a three wheeler in which to ride up and down the promenade. Extending my line of thought to the train journey to and from Abergele,I became aware that this too had played a major part in contributing to the best two weeks of my whole life. Like the trams of Manchester, they too represented the same family of mechanical giants, whose noisy rumblings beckoned instant conversion to the big world of steam and engineering contraptions. "Strange!, I can't see any trams yet." Diverting my attention back to the immediate present,and especially to the roadway in front of the bus,I peered through the window in search of my favourite transport where,in the hazy sunshine,my only reward was an outline of the empty tram tracks. "It can't be much further to Piccadilly,can it?" I had absolutely no idea of my whereabouts and geographically speaking,I was completely lost. "Mind you,anywhere outside the Styal boundary and a good three miles hence,was virgin territory so to speak." Talking to myself under my breath and reshuffling myself to a more comfortable position, I allowed my thoughts to drift once more in the opposite direction,or more appropiately, to the classroom where my pals would be begining their new term. My friend Oakbob,so went the story,had been discharged some weeks before me and was now living in a place called Levenshulme whereas Wooksie,according to my reckoning,would not qualify for release until next year. "I can just imagine him standing in front of the stage and trying his best to sing to the words of Nymphs and Shepherds." At this thought, I managed a wide grin,remembering the severity of Smiggy's intense protection of this,his beloved piece of music. "Wonder whose taken over the school captaincy?" This reflection, a reminder of my own circumstances,took me back to the last term's involvement when,in complete surprise,I was nominated for this prestigious position. Wearing the jacket of the school captain had enabled me to complete my education in a very relaxed atmosphere and with the punishments now a thing of the past,at least for me personally,the way forward bloss -omed into a kind of freedom only available to those with ex -perience and age. Included in this so called freedom, was the ability to make unnanounced entrances through doors and classrooms which came under my jurisdiction as chief messen-ger come skivvy,a privilege which was unique amongst school prefects and captains alike. Having infiltrated the upper sanctuary of teachers and staff rooms,I became conversant with grown-ups personal habits and conversation and such was the confidentiality entrusted to me,I enjoyed a freedom that seemed totally alien to anything I had ever known. A few of my encounters with individual teachers had not only subscri-bed to my education of the human race but had also made me more aware of being grown up,even to the point of misguided-ly including myself as one of those superior beings. In the case of the headmaster,I had cautiously come to accept his military style uniqueness as being his way of holding on to a discipline stretching as far back as his army career,a fac -t which was self evident by the way in which he carried his stick under his arm. My casual observance of Smiggy had re-mained a subject that I regarded as being taboo,especially since I preferred to continue keeping on the right side of him. However,one or two incidents concerning him and his be -haviour had lingered just long enough to cause a mild reac-tion and at least two of them had come as a total surprise. I remembered thinking on a few occasions,why ,it was necessary for him to play the piano with a female teacher sat on his knee and more recently,why he should repeat the process with a young girl from one of the girls' classrooms.

One of my first duties around the time of my fourteenth birthday,and one which causes me to reflect on my stupidity,was when the older boys of the school under my leadership,were instructed to march along the road and down Twinney's Brow, in order to fill-in the crater left by Styals' wartime bomb. In the morning sunshine,the troop,complete with gardening spades,arrived at the water filled hole for what had been jokingly diagnosed as a few fun filled hours off school work. In this relaxed setting adjacent to the National Trust,it be-came difficult even for me,to take the job in hand seriously,and before long,I too was an accomplice in the hilarity which was deemed to be a work experience. The apex of my irresponsibility came about when I accidently trod on one of the numerous cow pats scattered over the meadow,and taking my boot off in order to wash it in the crater,I leaned out with it balanced precariously on a piece of wood. Unfortunately,in my attempt to save myself from the mud slide,I had to let go of my boot in order to scramble to safety and in doing so, I left behind a floating boot that resembled some kind of ancient sailing barge. Amid howls of laughter and a barrage of name calling,I glanced at my personal belonging which had by this time edged its way towards the centre of the pool. The outcome in terms of boyish behaviour,was obvious and in no time,a spate of stone and mud throwing began in an effort to guide its drift to the sides. Within a few seconds of the bombardment,my possession began to sink beneath the muddy water and as it did so,it left behind a big solitary bubble as if to proclaim an epitaph on the site of its watery grave. Apart from the usual grumpy reaction from the footwear manager,and an accusation of cheating the Manchester Education Committee out of their property,the affair eventually subsided,but not without howls of laughter whenever reference was made about my boots. As a result of my foolishness concerning this sequence of events,a new lease of life was given to the 'Jimmy Brown' repertoire of rhyme, and looking back as if it were yesterday,I can still hear a musical chant from my so-called pals as they accompanied me to school and back; "Jimmy Brown, Jimmy Brown, washed his shoe before it drowned." This,my own final contribution,lingered just long enough for me to dwell on the scene at Bluebell Woods as I smilingly watched my old boot,threaded with a piece of string instead of a shoe lace,fill up with water before sinking. "Oh! well, at least there will always be a part of me for ever at Styal,even if it is only an old boot.

It wasn't so much as counting the days leading into the year ahead of me,but as each month became ticked off the calendar so too was there an awareness of finality to the closing stages of my youth. "This time next year,I'll probably be living in Manchester,or somewhere." This,just one of the many thoughts concerning the future,became tinted with traces of nostalgia as I contemplated the freedom ahead of me. "If my girlfriend is let out the same time as me,we can go to the pictures together,somewhere in Manchester,and sit on the row at the back,that way,I can put my arm around her and feel her shapely contours." My mind continued to run riot as I allowed my imagination to have a free reign,and seemingly, once I was in the city,the possibilities would become like a merry-go-round. "Jimmy Brown. Go and collect your belongings and report to 'E' Home. You're leaving us today." Miss Royden's instructions and my own anticipaton of the move to the 'big' boys home was the signal that I had reached the last chapter of my institutionalism and no doubt my next order would be to leave the colony of Styal forever. 'E' Home, in terms of work routines,was no different from the one I'd just left and as regards my privacy and the use of private lockers,they too were non existent. "I shall have to find a secret hiding place for my stamp collection and also another hideaway for my money." Thoughts of how I had put my hand up the fireplace chimney to retrieve my worldly wealth of three shillings and sixpence ha'penny,and getting covered in soot in the process,brought a smile to my face as I pondered over the future of my possessions. What was so different a -bout my new home was being under a joint leadership of man and woman,a married couple,who both shared in the administrations of every order and every job of work. Following my promotion,a wave of rumours had circulated the colony concerning the new successors to the retiring bandmaster's family,and with a certain amount of intrepidation I anxiously awaited my first confrontation. My nervousness was the end product of the many descriptions attributed to Mr Boston,the new administrator,and the comments concerning his profile were the reasons behind a renewal of my apprehensiveness. "He's a Sergeant Major who's just left the Army", said one of the older boys. "He's one of those drill instructors who always carries a stick like Smiggy", said another lad. Before the day had finished and all speculation run its course, the new administrators took up their post and chose the evening meal as being the ideal opportunity to introduce themselves. Everything about Mr Boston was,according to my mental picture,representative of how an ex segeant major would look and act when out of uniform. His height,combined with his heavy features,proclaimed a superiority that defied anyone to interrupt whilst he was talking,let alone look elsewhere during the lecture. In spite of Mr Boston's attempts at being a civilian head of the household,his military background and the clean-cut image -including his thick black manicured moustache- was an everyday reminder of a no-nonsence approach to discipline,where fear and reprisal for misbehaviour became constant companions. On reflection, that first encounter with the new disciplinarian wasn't exactly a fearful experience in view of the relaxed introductions by him and his wife but to the more mischievious and adventurous like myself,the underlying threat of a military style reprisal became another unwelcome hurdle on an already overcrowded circuit. During one of my intense periods of mental activity whilst viewing the Bollin valley from my hideout, I had asked myself why it was that Manchester Corporation always sent men with army or military backgrounds to look after children,and boys in particular. Feeling resentful over this and other issues concerning child welfare in which I be -came convinced of Manchesters' disregard of childrens real needs, I switched attentions to the new overseers and more es -pecially, to Mrs Boston. Her cooking, in my own opinion, was without doubt the best I had ever tasted but even this attri -bution became insufficient to include her amongs my favour- ite home mothers. It was probably because her looks and man -nerisms resembled those of Miss Thomalis, the homemother who had beaten me up, that blighted any warm feeling towards her although apart from that there was no other reason to pro- nounce an opinion on someone performing their duties under the shadow of a powerful partner. One particular incident, and one which highlighted Mrs Boston's inexperience and tim- idness, was when, probably due to an inability and frustration, she recruited her husband's authority to sort out a problem of what to her, was of a very delicate nature. I remembered that particular incident and the sheepish looks on the boys faces if only for its surprise and embarrassment. On the day in question, or more appropiately, on the night in quest -ion, the whole dormitory was awakened by the noise of a long stick being rattled across the rows of iron bedsteads and un -der the glare of bright lights, the angry voice of Mr Boston reverberated within the four walls. "Throw your top covers back and stand to attention by your beds." Standing menacing -ly in the doorway in front of his wife, he continued; "I am not going to make any excuses for this interruption. Most of you know why I am here. If you think I'm going to let my wife put up with this filthy habit day in and day out, you're sadly mistaken. From now on,I shall personally inspect your bedding every day and those who have been making tents under their sheets,will have me to answer to." Following their departure and 'lights out',the bedroom came alive to whispered remarks and giggles until finally,having exhausted a plentiful supply of appropiate comments,peace and quietness reigned once more. Before nodding off myself,I had experien -ced a few guilty feelings of shame but having reasoned to my own satisfaction the whys and wherefores,I concluded that it wasn't our fault,but theirs. "What else was there to do; in bed for nine o'clock,lights out,and still wide awake?"

School had become very boring during my last term,with my up -permost thoughts concentrating more on the future than the present. Girls,as usual,were dominating most of my leisure time and especially with one particular girl,who's voluptous figure and serene-like shyness contributed to a make-believe courtship of unprecedented horizons. "If only we could go to the pictures together." This,just one of my many fantasies, became an immediate reality when she accepted my courageous offer to take her to the Rex cinema on the Saturday afternoon. Reflecting on this,and on how briefly the love affair had lasted,I relived my moment of glory on the back row and on how my fingers had traced the full roundedness of her big breasts beneath the fabric before eventually cupping them in my hands. "Stop it! Stop it! You're just like all the other boys. You're only after me for one thing." My indignation at being accused of this terrible thing,even if it was true, settled on my shoulders and reduced my exploring during the remainder of the matinee,to a mere holding of hands. The countdown to my eventual last day at school began after the Easter recess with every single week representing a closer link to my eventual discharge. "In a funny sort of way", I remembered thinking at one stage,"mine's a similar situation to one of those prisoners in an old black and white picture, where,on the wall of his cell,he ticks off the day and weeks to the time of his release." Styal, so far as I was concer -ned,would always represent a prison establishment,and even allowing for any of the good times, fear,oppression and dep- rivation,would always be the front runners to any future mem -ories. Almost as if announcing my final countdown, a Spit- fire zoomed past the windows of the school one day and bur- ied itself in the ploughed field next to the building,a spot normally occupied by the potato pickers during the harvest season. That display of heroism by the school teacher was my last recollection of a school which had contributed to so many bad memories,and surveying the damage to the trees of Shaw's Fold as I made my way back to the Homes, I recalled the precise moment in which the teacher had made his dash to rescue the pilot.

Prior to my final leaving of the school,there had been one particular ceremony in which the school leavers had been al- lowed to put on display,the creation of their final terms' handywork,and the result of my own endeavour,was a hand car- ved jewellery box made from oak. I had felt justifiably pr- oud of my achievement even to the point of showing off the polished casket to all and sundry of my male and female pals who were equally engrossed in the same ego boosting exercise with their own accomplishments. What to do with the casket and who to give it to,had been decided as far back as the first groove by my tenon saw,and hopefully,if Vera comes to visit me before I get let-out,I will present it to her for a keepsake. The ever increasing noise of traffic,together with the still continuing dark haze above,seemed to signify that the city centre wasn't too far away. Transferring the paper parcel to my lap and holding it by the coarse string, I peered out of the window in expectation of sighting a Manchester tram which,to my way of thinking,should be making an appearance any time now. "Concilio et Labore." Talking to myself in whispered tones, I repeated the latin words of the motto which boldly emphasised the Manchester coat of arms; "Concilio et Labore." I had lived with the same motto for almost every day of my life especially during the schooldays when the emblem had stared back at me from every school book every pencil,and everything else associated with my mentors. Having seen the same motto at least half a dozen times along my route into the city,I was reminded of how much my life had been influenced by the latter part of the slogan and how ignorant I was of its true meaning. Giving a momentary feel to the contents of my brown paper parcel reminded me of what had transpired this very morning,a drama that had not only left me feeling destitute,but one that had introduced me to the world of true pauperism. When the Superintendant had ordered me to collect my belongings,it became the signal for me to extract from my hiding places,the only two possessions of my entire life. Filled with all the excitement of the day ahead,I first went to the fireplace in my bedroom where, in a tiny alcove inside the chimney breast,I had hidden my savings of seven shillings and ninepence ha'penny. Unsuccess -ful at the first attempt,I continued to grope in all directions until there was nowhere else to search. At that point the frightening prospect of it having disappeared,suddenly dawned on me. "It's gone! Somebody's pinched my savings." With so little time left in which to prepare for my release I realized how hopeless the situation was. Cursing inwardly behind an expression already damp from stray tears,I blasphemed at the whole of the Styal institution and especially at the system responsible for my present state of hopelessness. My only consolation was the fact that at least,my own personal stamp collection was in a safe hiding place. Having removed all traces of soot,I set off dressed in my new suit in the direction of the shoe repair shop,a route which took me through the workyard enclosure. "Good luck,lad. I hear you're leaving us today." With an outstretched arm,Mr Lyle shook my hand warmly with a gesture that took me by surprise "My!, you do look a gentleman in those long trousers." It always seemed strange to me that Amos Lyle,just an ordinary workman in a boiler suit,always seemed to know what was going on in the colony. Continuing my line of thought, I reck -oned to myself that of all the people in authority at the Homes,he was the only one to have shown any kind of feelings towards me. What made him different,I wasn't sure,but there was a sense of understanding about him that made me feel he shared and embraced at least,a small portion of my life. It was obvious that there was something in common between Amos Lyle and myself because only a few weeks ago,when practicing my poetry writing,I had written a verse concerning him. It was only a short verse,and that was the reason for remembering it so well. It went; "Once upon a time in Styal, lived a man called Amos Lyle, Old and wise and kind at heart, Gives us rides on'th horse and cart."

Above the noise of hammering which greeted me as I made my entrance into the shoe shop,I shouted a friendly hello! at the manager,expecting in return,a warm reaction to the obvious signs of my departure. His sour expression remained intact as he pointed to his associate. "He's over there. He'll be with you in a minute." Smilingly,I explained my circumstances to the young assistant,pointing out that I had only ten minutes in which to walk to the bus stop for the journey to Manchester. In anticipation of his help,I shyly waited for the sign that indicated he was about to retrieve the album from our shared hiding place. With an explanation about having too much work to stop what he was doing,he pointed to the drawer under the work bench and told me to look for the stamp collection myself. Sliding back the heavy drawer, I reached under the brown paper covering and felt for the familiar shape of my album. There was nothing there but an emptiness. "It must be a prank. He's probably hidden it somewhere else to make me panic." My thoughts came to an abrupt end as I delved into the remaining two drawers,hoping to God that it was in one of them. The first hint of a growing suspicion loomed ever closer as I completed my search of the second drawer and with only one to go,my pulse rate multiplied to the same pace as my increasing panic. With nothing but empty drawers to show for my efforts,I looked up at him from across the room,my questioning expression seeking an answer to my show of despair and devastation. "What's-up, can't you find it? It was there yesterday. I haven't touched it; honest to God." Even before he had finished the sentence I knew what the outcome to the crisis would be.and having digested what up until a few moments ago,was almost unthinkable,I begrudgingly faced up to the inevitable acceptance of utter defeat. My sixth sense told me that it would be futile to try and question someone older and more experienced in life than me and in any case,there just wasn't the time. What should have been my finest hour, a farewell full of rewards in return for a lifetimes' endeavours and hard labour, had now turned into a tragic comedy where an unimaginable situation had reduced my personal possessions and wealth to an absolute zero. Looking back to this mornings' drama,and to the sorrow that had tinted my day, I remembered my reaction as I walked out of the gates for the last time, and the thought that came to me of not only being alone in the world,but having to begin a new life without a penny to my name. "Oh,well!" I remembered thinking to myself; "I came in to Styal Homes with nothing,and now I'm going out with nothing."

"I wonder if my pals enjoyed the summer holiday this year? If I hadn't been too old and awaiting my discharge,I would have gone to Lake Windemere with them." This,my concluding thought about Styal,was cut short as I viewed what appeared to be a traffic congestion ahead. The speed of the bus had almost slowed to a walking pace,thus providing me with an op -portunity to scan the streets and buildings on both sides of the vehicle,and through the mid-day haze a large hoarding advertizing the 'Ink Spots' came into view. "I wonder what the 'Ink Spots' are? Maybe it's the title of a show or one of those musicals I'd heard about." A few minutes later,the bus drew into the terminus at Piccadilly Gardens and all of a sudden I was aware of the finality of my journey. "I wasnt just visiting Manchester; I was returning to start a new be-gining in the city I had been born in where,in normal circum -stances,I might have had a reception party of friends and family to greet me." As it was, my vulnerability and ignor-ance of what was going on all about me,made me feel like a tiny speck in a claustrophobic metropolis where busy people, tall buildings,and noisy traffic,contributed to my state of growing insecurity. After a few moments of waiting on the pavement,clutching a parcel that had nervously changed hands at least a dozen times, I was interrupted by the words; "are you Jimmy Brown?" Nodding attentively in reply,I waited in anticipation of what was about to be revealed concerning my future. "My name,is Mr Crossley. I'm a Childrens' Officer for Manchester City Council and I, am going to be in charge of your welfare. First of all, we've got to find you some-where to live,and then,later on, find a suitable job of work for you to do." Indicating that this would be an appropiate moment in which to deal with the business in hand,he opened his briefcase and took out a sheaf of papers. "Would you like a cup of tea? "I'll go and buy us both one whilst you find one of the benches to sit on." After returning the cup to the tea caravan I resumed my sitting position in front of the manicured gardens,where I continued to gaze in awe at so many things I had never seen before. "Why don't you speak? Have you nothing to say? Surely there must be something you want to ask." I was speechless for one reason only. I felt completely out of my depth,with nothing in common with any-thing,or anybody,and even if I did have a viewpoint,I was far too shy to make a comment. "Your sister Vera couldn't take the time off work,otherwise she would have been here to meet you." After digesting his remark,I directed my line of vision towards the terminus and,to the one subject that had been uppermost in my mind since leaving Styal. "I wonder if I could ask him about the trams?" I hadn't seen any sign of them so far and I was growing impatient at the delay. "Perhaps they're all out in service at the moment and not due back till this afternoon." Unable to contain myself any longer,I waited until he had finished his sentence concern-ing my clothing and other items,and then,summoning up a cour-age from out of nowhere,I opened my mouth. "Excuse me,Sir, where are all the trams?" Mr Crossley began to chuckle and then,broke into a burst of laughter. "What trams? lad!" His composure,having returned to a more serious side,displayed a tiny hint of concern as he continued: "Didn't you know? I thought everybody knew. They've all been burned,every last one of them." If his temperament hadn't become more sober, I would have taken his hilarity to be some kind of mischievous attempt at getting me to react but as it was,his depiction of sincerity became so convincing, that fear replaced every other feeling in my body. I was too frightened to ackknowledge what he had said,just in case he had passed on the wrong information,and yet,after a moment of thought,I reluctantly accepted that his revelation explained the absence of any of the Manchester trams. A silent anger began to take a hold of me as I reflected on all the years of secret longing and on all the imaginary journeys I had hoped would one day become a reality. The half of me that refused to believe Mr Crossley,also questioned the feasibility of a bonfire containing all the trams. "Surely,nobody would set fire to all those beautiful red and white trams?" Interrupting my blank stare,the Children's Officer said: "I'm sorry,son, were you thinking of having a ride on a tram?" In complete shock at the tragic news, and at a catastrophe that had caused yet more unhappiness, I nodded my head in acknowledgement."Cheer up lad, its not the end of the world. Now then, we're going to take you on a bus to where you're going to live. Its a place called Levenshulme,not far from where your sister Vera lives. You'll like it there. The Mother of the house has a son a little older than you and he plays the bugle in a Boys Brigade. Isn't that what you used to play?" My continuing silence, due to the shock of learning about 'my' trams, was begining to irritate him as I again shook my head. "What's wrong with you. Can't you talk about anything? A boy like you,and of your age,should be into all sorts of things. How about a hobby? Surely you've got a hobby." The theft of my stamp collection sprang painfully to mind as I mentally anguished at his insensitivity and bad timing. Trying his best to encourage me into conversation,he said: "Do you know,I've got a son of my own who's only five years old, and he can tell you every different model of car that's made." This re -vellation did nothing to cheer me up or gain my interest. All it achieved,was to make me feel resentful towards him for making me feel stupid and unintelligent. "Where I came from,there weren't any cars to see,and who,if anybody, was going to tell us about vehicles,when they were all too busy doing their jobs of work." This,a silent reflection on an interview that was descending into a silent question and answer routine,was ended by a different question,and one which made a lot more sense. "Would you like a sandwich from the refreshment caravan?" At this,my interest suddenly came to life and taking the money he had offered,I walked through the gardens feeling full of importance,as I prepared to make my first ever purchase in the city of Manchester.

By the time my Childrens' Officer had deposited me at my new home,a small terraced house in a street somewhere between Cromwell Grove and Broom Lane, I had retrieved my usual sense of optimism and now,instead of the forlorness of the past few hours,an eagerness for what my future fate might hold,be -gan to shine through. During the bus ride to Levenshulme, I had learned from Mr Crossley the correct way of purchasing a travel ticket,in addition to noting the numbers of the bus in case I became lost in the city. Ever since achieving my school scholarship,I had been aware of my talent for writing and composition and it had always been my ambition to become involved in a job that included my favourite subject. For some unknown reason,when Mr Crossley asked me what I wanted to do,regarding my future,my assumption was such, that because I didn't think I was good enough or intelligent enough to be involved in office work,I settled for the alternative which was being an electrician. After a further discussion and an indepth explanation of how I was to hand over my wage packet to my new mother who,in turn,would deduct all her expenses and leave me with approximately five or six shillings a week with which to spend how I liked, he returned to his important looking paper-work before completing his business with my new mother. "By the way, don't leave the house this evening; your sister Vera is coming round to see you after tea." This,his final comment,seemed to act as a final farewell to my past life as I mentally prepared myself for not only my immediate future,once the door had closed on him,but for a life that was going to be so very different to the one I had known until today. At first sight,Mrs Mathewson appeared to be an old grey haired lady who expressed the burden of life in her every mannerism. Remembering what Mr Crossley had said about me treating her as a mother, and she treating me as another son, I began to sense that in spite of her being in need of an extra income to supplement her widowhood, she was genuine as a person and genuine about my future welfare. After showing me around the house,she offered me the opportunity of spending some time in my 'own' room,whilst she got on with preparing for tonights' dinner. This interlude of peace and quiet,and a moment in which to put my life into perspective,was never more welcome as I sat down hesitantly on one side of the single bed. The bedroom, a small space of cluttered objects of furniture,including a dark oak -like wardrobe, a chest of drawers, and a bed with a similar dark wood headboard, became suddenly,overbearing and claustrophobic. In such a tiny space,even with its new wallpaper and paint,it was only a fraction of the size of my previous dormitory and my immediate reaction was to open the window over-looking the alleyway and back yard. Breathing in some fresh air and returning to my bedside,I became conscious of the fact that I had a bedroom all to myself and what's more, I would be sleeping on my own for the very first time. "How was I going to fill those drawers,let alone a wardrobe? I only possess a spare set of underclothes,a shirt,a suit, and a pair of shoes. They'll look lost in all the empty spaces in the drawers and wardrobe." According to Mrs Mathewson, dinner,tonight,would be at five thirty,but in the meantime there would be a snack of tea and cakes,once she had organized herself. Feeling the effects of all that had transpired, and my mind working overtime on all aspects of the days' events,I leaned against the high pillows and stretched out to sink down onto a bed of exceptional comfort. It wasn't long before the inevitable comparisons between Styal and Manchester occupied my mind and almost as soon as the process began to gain momentum,I found myself drifting through the sunny meadows and wallowing in the sheer magnetism of the Bollin Valley. Only one thing marred my reminiscing, and that, was the nightmare of the Manchester trams burning beyond recognition and subsequently leaving behind a pyre of skeletons of twisted blackened metal. By the time I had regained consciousness,the pillow had absorbed a hundred tears or more, such,was the dampness of the fabric, and whether the watery outburst during my snooze had been a reaction to a new kind of contentment at finally having a home of my own,or at the demise of my cherished Manchester trams, I will never know. There was a strange kind of sadness linked to almost everything that had transpired today and whether this was attributable to the transition from past to present,was beyond me. Maybe it was the realization that 'Jimmy Wish Wish', now no longer a part of my life, had finally given way to the more appropiate and realistic,'Jimmy Brown, went to town'. With a continuing fear and uncertainty about my immediate future, and an overwhelming sense of being alone in the world, I continued to wipe my eyes and blow my nose in the handkerchief that Matron had given me this morning. Such,were the powerful feelings of emotion now threatening to engulf me, I was reminded of the time I had sobbed helplessly in the arms of Miss Chedley. In my present state of mind,the temptation to collapse in despair,was only a hairsbreadth away,and just as if God,in his wisdom,had despatched an angel to rescue the situation,the saintly-like Mrs Mathewson walked quietly into my room,holding a cup and saucer in one hand and a biscuit tin in the other. "Thought you might need cheering up" she said,as she placed the items on the dressing table. My show of gratitude,and the uncontrollable urge to give expression to a whole fathom of pent-up emotion, must have indicated that it was just the right time for her to intervene. Placing herself next to me on the bed,she placed one arm a-round my shoulder and using the same quiet tone of voice, said; "come now Jimmy, or is it James; what is it that is troubling you and making you so sad? Come on, tell me all about it." With that, the dam burst.

THE END

Sylvia Stanhope as Miss Manchester.

STYAL, HOMES.
I suppose you dont know this place.
J. H. BAYLEY, WILMSLOW.

Styal Cottage Homes Entrance.

THE VILLAGE.
HOLLIN LANE
WAR MEMORIAL.
STYAL
THE OLD SHIP INN
BOLLIN VALLEY.

CRUMPSALL WORKHOUSE

Manchester's last tram at Slade Lane Manchester 1949.

My sister Vera with *The Box* I made at school.

A recent photo of myself and my sister Vera.

E P I L O G U E

Some years later, in spite of being advised against delving into her past, Vera Brown made the breakthrough she had been praying for ever since leaving the orphanage. The words: "Jimmy, I've found our Mother" were the crowning rewards to many months of persistent determination in seeking to re-unite the family, and for a brief moment in time, the ensuing euphoria gave rise to an elation that spelled success for the moment and hope for the future. Unfortunately, it soon became apparent that a family life together was very much out of the question, since 'Mother's Home' turned out to be the Workhouse at Crumpsall, in North Manchester, the place she had lived at, ever since 1936. In todays' world of modern medicines, her illness, one associated with a type of post natal milk infection, would inevitably have been curable. As it was, her admittance to Crumpsall Hospital spelled the begining of a life sentence from which there was no escape, and like most inmates of a workhouse, she was put to work in order for her to earn her keep. Sylvia, my mother, one of the oldest survivors of the famed Crumpsall Workhouse, died peacefully at the ripe old age of 94 years, at Lancaster Moor Hospital.

My sister Vera, the younger of the two, lived happily with the same foster Mother in Levenshulme up until her marriage. She and her husband now live a life of retirement after a lifetime's partnership and continue to share in the involvement of their four children.

E P I L O G U E (2)

Sylvia, my elder sister, was eventually adopted by an ageing childless couple from North Manchester, who saw in her natural beauty, an opportunity to become a part of the social 'set', whilst promoting their own ambitions. This partnership was to last for a decade or more, during which time, Sylvia, influenced by the seemingly ever generous parents, became a part of the Manchester scene and a member of the eletist social fraternity. Successful in her own business career, Sylvia's moment of triumph occurred during the early 1950's when, as 'Miss Manchester', she progressed to the finals of the 'Miss U.K. Beauty Competition at Blackpool, Regrettably, the other side of the coin revealed a great unhappiness and, an intense suffocation which caused her to flee her native Manchester. Because of this episode, she sought a new life abroad and eventually married a Swiss/ Frenchman before settling down in Paris. Sylvia's untimely death in the 1970's, came as a great shock to her family and not least, to her two young daughters, who were left to cope at a vulnerable age. Her three surviving children, now live in the North West and in Europe.

As for myself; that will have to wait until another episode!